The Philosophy of Language

MITCHELL S. GREEN

New York   Oxford

OXFORD UNIVERSITY PRESS

Oxford University Press is a department of the University of Oxford.
It furthers the University's objective of excellence in research, scholarship,
and education by publishing worldwide. Oxford is a registered trademark of
Oxford University Press in the UK and certain other countries.

Published in the United States of America by Oxford University Press,
198 Madison Avenue, New York, NY 10016, United States of America.

© 2021 by Oxford University Press

CIP data is on file at the Library of Congress
978-0-19-085304-4

Printing number: 9 8 7 6 5 4 3 2 1
Printed by LSC Communications, United States of America

To my mother
Isabel Green
who said I could be anything

BRIEF CONTENTS

....

v

CONTENTS

....

FIGURES, TABLES, AND BOXES

....

PREFACE

I have three aims in writing this book. First, I hope to give undergraduate and graduate students new to the philosophy of language, as well as researchers who want a refresher on the subject, a compact and reasonably current overview of the field. For this purpose the book is self-contained, with numerous pointers both to classic texts and highlights of contemporary research. At the end of each chapter, readers will find suggestions for further reading that would enable them to bring their understanding to a more advanced level. That is also where readers will find study questions they may use to test and deepen their understanding of that chapter's material.

A second aim of the book is to showcase some of what has gone right in philosophy over the last 150 years. Students new to philosophy as well as kibitzers who might have only dabbled in it often criticize the field on the ground that it does not make progress. We are, after all, still debating some of the same questions that vexed Plato and Aristotle! However, that complaint may belie a failure to recognize another aspect of the discipline. Philosophers work in the basement of the house of knowledge. Occasionally they find something of interest down there, polish it up, repair it a little if needed, and then hand it upstairs for someone of a more applied or empirical bent to use. Since the mid-nineteenth century, philosophers have paid attention to everyday experience surrounding meaning and in some rudimentary degree begun theorizing about it. I have in mind accounts of such things as entailment, quantification, reference, presupposition, implicature, speaker meaning, and common ground. Each of these notions was given an initial characterization by philosophers or logicians, whose work in turn helped to support the development of areas of modern linguistics concerned with syntax and semantics.[1] As well, linguists and psychologists have taken up some of these notions and made them experimentally tractable. We now have experimental pragmatics, for instance, putting competing pragmatic hypotheses to empirical test. These developments together suggest that when my field does its work well, it contributes to our understanding of one of our species' signal achievements: language.

A third aim of the book, continuous with the second, is to help readers cultivate greater self-knowledge. Given the importance of language to most of our lives, sharpening our insight into it may help to shed light on what occurs within our minds, and between conversing minds, on an everyday basis. As a student of language for over three decades, I've been struck by how often people seem unaware of when they are speaking metaphorically, of how easy it is for their words to be misconstrued, and of how effortlessly they mean more than they say. We sometimes unwittingly hurt others with toxic language, and we can have our words silenced, or at least muted, in ways that may easily go undetected. Philosophers of language have been reflecting on these phenomena and have offered theories that may shed light on how they occur. I hope that by sharing some of these developments I may help you open up parts of your life that were difficult to detect with the naked ear.

I am indebted to the following teachers and colleagues (not all of whom are still with us) for insights, challenges, skepticism, and encouragement over many years that have helped me to better understand the Philosophy of Language: Dorit Bar-On, Nuel Belnap, Robert Brandom, Joseph Camp, Michael Dummett, Michael Kubovy, Bill Lycan, John McDowell, John Searle, Keith Simmons, Rich Thomason, and John Williams. I have also been blessed with excellent students who have made me rethink some of my field's most fundamental assumptions. Among them are Emma Bjorngard-Basayne, Ralph DiFranco, Corin Fox, Jordan Ochs, Andrew Morgan, and Michael Pelczar. For careful comments on earlier drafts of this book, I would like to thank Marianna Bergamaschi, Bianca Cepollaro, Brady Clark, Jan Michel, Andrew Morgan, and Michael Schmitz. Lori Green's love, patience, and support

---

1. Goldsmith and Laks's *Battle in the Mindfields* (University of Chicago Press, 2019) traces some important steps in this history.

made the writing of this book a great deal more pleasant than it would otherwise have been. Clementine and I walked hundreds of miles while discussing the topics of this book, though admittedly conversation may have been a bit one-sided.

Note to Instructors

This book is designed to be useful as a text for an undergraduate Philosophy of Language course or for a survey-level graduate course in that field. It does not presuppose previous coursework in philosophy, logic, or linguistics, and I have been at pains to present the material in the most accessible and intuitive way I know how. I have also aimed to give readers a sense of exploring questions *with* me rather than having it presented to them as a body of established fact. (Some of the field is, of course, comparatively established, but my experience suggests that students learn it more effectively if we can motivate even those views we take to be settled.)

Instructors may wish to assign some of the study questions at the end of each chapter as brief writing assignments, or as talking points to inspire in-class discussion. Also, at the end of each chapter, I've identified a small number of readings that, due to their historical significance or extraordinary lucidity, could usefully be paired with those chapters. Although this text could be used by itself for an academic quarter or semester, it could also be supplemented with any of those further readings at the instructor's discretion. In addition, with the aid of these resources, an instructor could design a Philosophy of Language course with one or another orientation. Among these are the following:

Philosophy of Language with an orientation toward semantics: Emphasize Chapters 2–5 and pair these with Altshuler et al. (2019) cited in Chapter 3.

A historically oriented course in Philosophy of Language: Emphasize Chapters 1–4 and pair these with cited works of Plato, Aristotle, Locke, and Rousseau, Frege, Russell, Ayer, or Wittgenstein.

Philosophy of Language with an orientation toward pragmatics: Emphasize Chapters 3–6 and pair these with readings from Austin, Grice, Searle, Bach, and Recanati.

Philosophy of Language with an orientation toward social and political philosophy or feminism: Emphasize Chapters 5–8 and pair these with readings from Langton, Hornsby, Hom, Jeshion, Maitra, or Saul.

Ancillaries

The Oxford University Press Ancillary Resource Center (ARC) at oup-arc.com houses an Instructor's Manual with Test Bank and PowerPoint Lecture Outlines for instructor use. Student resources are also available on the ARC and include self-quizzes, flashcards, media activities, and links to helpful material on the Internet. These materials are available at oup.com/he/green1e

CHAPTER 1

Meaning
Varieties, Aspects, and Sources

Chapter Overview

One central feature of language is meaning. Yet because it is used in a wide range of ways in everyday and scientific discourse, the concept of meaning can be puzzling. In this chapter we will distinguish some of the more important uses of the notion and isolate those that are most pertinent to communication in our own and other species. We will then formulate eleven aspects of communicative meaning and briefly consider some prominent theories of its origins. We will also clarify some of the ways in which Philosophy of Language differs from Linguistics and how in this book we will be using the notion of language.

1.1. Some Varieties of Meaning

Suppose that while chatting with a friend in a café, you happen to mention the effort you've put into growing kale in your neighborhood's community garden. She now replies,

1.1. How's that working out for you?

She has clearly asked a question and has used meaningful words in doing so. But you might also wonder whether she is being a tad sarcastic in asking that question. Is there a bit of saltiness that goes beyond her words? Yet you may hesitate to ask her if there is, since in so doing you might reveal some naïveté.

You've also probably wondered, at some point, what a dog means in wagging its tail or in barking. How about birdsong? Is it just for the sake of making a din that wakes you up on a spring morning, or are those birds communicating in some way? And if so, what if anything are they *saying* to each other? Likewise, is the sweet fragrance of a hyacinth flower in full bloom a kind of invitation to potential pollinators— a floral, "Come hither!"—or is the analogy with invitations in our own species too far-fetched?

You may have wondered as well whether it is possible to refer to things that, at least on the face of it, do not exist. It seems clear that when I say,

1.2. No one is coming down the road,

a listener is at best making a bad joke in replying, "Well, was he walking slowly or quickly?" However, the subject of that sentence is apparently 'No one,' and so we might still wonder how (1.2) can be true unless it refers to something—perhaps a mysterious and ethereal entity? Again,

1.3. Kronos devoured his children,

seems to be meaningful: at least if we have some familiarity with Greek mythology, we seem to know what someone who utters this sentence is saying. But how can that be unless the name 'Kronos' refers to an individual, and the rest of the sentence says, of that individual, that he devoured his children? Does this line of thought suggest that just by reasoning about language we can deduce that the ancient Greeks were right about the existence of their deities after all? That would be quite a hat-trick!

In this book we will examine questions such as these three, and while we will not arrive at definitive answers to them all, I hope to provide you with tools for making progress in your thinking about the variety of forms that meaning can take and how those forms relate to one another. Where appropriate, I will also point you to current research that investigates these questions in further depth than will be possible here. If all goes well, you will better understand the natural and social worlds around you and deepen your appreciation of your communication with others. You may even find that you occasionally mean more than you realize!

A bit of progress with the questions we raised earlier begins with noting that central to our subject matter is the phenomenon of *meaning as it relates to communication.* This phrase may sound redundant, perhaps like "basketball as it relates to sports" or "banking as it relates to the economy." What other kind of meaning could there be except that which relates to communication? In everyday thought and speech, however, we often make use of a notion of meaning that is not germane to communication. For instance, gazing out the window of the aforementioned café and gesturing toward the horizon your friend might remark:

1.4. Those dark clouds over there mean a storm is heading our way.

In so speaking, your friend is invoking what one philosopher has called "natural meaning" (Grice 1957). This notion concerns the way in which one object or state of affairs carries information about another object or state of affairs. Just as dark clouds mean rain, certain types of spots on a child's skin mean she has measles, and the pattern discernible in a cliff face means it has been subject to erosion due to wind coming from a certain direction. Yet clouds, spots on the skin, and configurations on a cliff are not, at least in the situations just described, in the business of communication: at most they are symptoms of some aspect of the world distinct from themselves. As such, these examples of natural meaning are cases of meaning that are not communicative.

According to a long tradition in Philosophy, any meaning that is germane to communication must be traceable back to one or more minds. Let us return again to the café scenario with which this chapter began. Imagine that as you ponder whether there was a veiled criticism in your friend's question (1.1), you also see someone a few tables away who appears to be winking at you. But you're not sure. After all, some winks just result from tics or errant dust particles. On the other hand, the owner of the winking eye seems intriguing. So you'd like to sort this out. Two possible explanations come to mind: he winked at you in order to get your attention, and possibly start up a conversation; or he did so because of a tic or a dust particle irritating his eye. The latter explanation, as you now know, is just an example of natural meaning and would presumably dash your hopes. On the other hand, the former type of wink would be due to his intending to get your attention. Since intending is a mental process or event, it is the kind of thing that many philosophers focus on as the source of communicative meaning.

That focus may be a bit myopic, however. There are forms of meaning germane to communication that do not result from intentions or other mental states. Biologists have discovered many cases in which nonhuman animals have traits or engage in behaviors that appear to mean something, in a sense that is richer than natural meaning as described earlier but still not involving intentions. One example comes from the humble millipede. Marek et al. (2011) have studied millipedes that start glowing when under threat of being attacked. It turns out millipedes that glow when in danger of predation are much more likely to deter predators than are those that do not. This suggests that the glowing is a signal meaning something like "Don't eat me, I'm poisonous!" As we shall see later, by calling a trait or behavior of an organism a signal, we mean more than that it conveys information: we mean that it is *designed* to convey information. And yet it doesn't seem terribly likely that millipedes intend to send signals to other creatures. The glowing might instead be a reaction triggered by their perception of a threat to their safety. That reaction might serve a purpose (just as my own spike in blood pressure serves to prepare me for a fight-or-flight response when I perceive a threat to my own safety), without being intended to do so.

Similarly, suppose that while all alone you happen to read something that makes you irritated. As you read on, you catch yourself scowling. But knowing that you are alone, you are probably not scowling with the intention of sending a message to someone else about your emotional condition. Yet at least according to one line of research on the psychology of human facial expressions, such expressions are designed to convey information about our emotional states (Keltner et al. 2003). Well, who "designs" such facial expression if not you? To answer this, notice that your body has many features designed to play certain roles: your heart is designed to pump blood, and your skin's job is to help regulate your body's temperature. We may shed light on how these traits have specific functions by appreciating that they likely conferred a survival advantage on our ancestors. Evolution through natural selection (ENS), however, is a wholly nonmental process. According to ENS, organisms are occasionally born with modifications in their genetic makeup producing features conferring a reproductive and/or survival advantage as compared with their siblings: longer legs that enable them to run faster, better wings for flight, or greater ability to resist disease. If a feature like one of these increases an organism's ability to survive, its likelihood of passing that feature to its offspring also increases (Charlesworth and Charlesworth 2017).

The foregoing style of explanation is what enables evolutionary biologists to think of traits that organisms possess as designed to perform certain jobs without those scientists having to suppose that such traits were produced by an intelligent or sentient designer. With that in mind, we may now observe that some traits and behaviors are designed not to pump blood or regulate body temperature but to convey information about an organism's potential toxicity, its emotional state, its readiness to mate, or readiness to attack. Let's call these traits and behaviors bearers of *organic meaning* to set them aside from the two other kinds we have considered so far. Accordingly we may distinguish three types:

1. *Natural meaning*: one entity or process carries information about a distinct entity or process. (Spots on the skin mean chicken pox; clouds on the horizon mean an approaching storm).
2. *Organic meaning*: one entity or process has a feature that is designed to carry information about a distinct entity or process. (The millipede's bioluminescence is designed to signal that it is poisonous; the human smile is designed to carry information about its owner's emotional state.) The design in question may, but need not, be the result of anyone's intentions.
3. *Speaker meaning*: one entity or process has a feature that is intentionally designed by an agent to carry information about a distinct entity or process. (Sydney's wink is intentionally designed to convey information about his interest in talking to you.)

Being designed intentionally is one way, but not the only way, in which a trait or object can play a certain role. As a result, speaker meaning, at least as it occurs in our species, is a special case of organic meaning. Both are germane to communication, while natural meaning is germane to communication insofar as it is a source from which evolutionary processes might yield organic meanings.[1] In addition to these three, we are now ready to add a fourth notion describing a property that words, phrases, and sentences have, namely,

4. *Linguistic meaning*: a word, phrase, or sentence has linguistic meaning just in case it has a relatively stable capacity to be used for saying things. (The sentence, 'Edison forgot to turn off the lights,' can, because of what it means, be used to say that Edison forgot to

---

1. An exception to this general pattern is in cases in which someone intentionally uses a naturally meaningful entity with the purpose of conveying information. I might, for instance, show a nurse my lacerated hand in order to get medical attention.

turn off the lights; a proper noun may be used to refer to someone, an adjective can be used to ascribe a characteristic to something being attended to, and so on for other parts of speech.)

Linguistic meaning has attracted enormous interest over the last 150 years, and it has inspired intricate and powerful theories in the process. It will be the focus of Chapters 2 and 3 and the background for much of our discussion thereafter.

In everyday conversation we also make use of a notion of meaning having to do with personal significance. Aromas can sometimes bring us back to moments in our past: the beach, watercolor paints, and certain dishes all exude aromas that are effective on me in this way. A tree in your grandmother's yard, textures, or songs from your childhood or teenage years, might have a similar power for you. It is natural to describe any of these cases with such words as "That song (aroma, tree, etc.) means so much to me." We thus have a fifth notion of meaning:

5. *Personal meaning*: An item (such as a natural phenomenon or artifact reminding you of your past) may have significance for you by virtue of its power to call up memories or other associations.

As important as personal meaning may be for an individual, it is not particularly relevant to communication. This is due in part to the fact that what is personally meaningful for me may not be for someone else. As a result, if I try to convey a message of great personal significance to someone else by, for instance, getting him to waft in an aroma that I associate with a happy moment in my childhood, he might be able to do no more than guess what I am trying to convey. Personal meanings only become communicative when they are shared among people with a rich common background of experience. As a result, they tend only to be useful for communication when other more basic communicative systems are in place.

We have considered five forms of meaning so far, and have suggested that types 1 (natural meaning) and 5 (personal meaning) will only be indirectly relevant to our concerns in this book. On the other hand, types 2–4 (organic meaning, speaker meaning, and linguistic meaning) will be central to what follows. These three constitute the main types of communicative meaning, and their relations are depicted in Figure 1.1, according to which the categories of linguistic meaning and speaker meaning are properly included within the broader category of organic meaning.

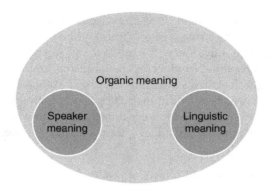

FIGURE 1.1 Venn diagram representing the relations among organic, speaker, and linguistic meaning

To better understand communicative meaning, let's set out some of its central aspects.

1.2. Eleven Aspects of Communicative Meaning

I mentioned earlier that linguistic meaning has been a topic of intensive research over the last century and a half, and as a result we do well to equip ourselves as soon as we can with tools for appreciating its power and complexity; we will also take note of some other aspects of communicative meaning along the way. Here we list and briefly characterize eleven aspects of communicative meaning.

CM1: Some words and sentences are meaningful; others are not

This point might seem too obvious to mention, but it turns out to be easy to lose sight of once we have entered the thickets of Philosophy of Language. So let us note that while a word such as 'triangularity' and the phrase 'My great aunt's favorite fountain pen' are meaningful expressions of English, the following are not:

> tulgey (a word that Lewis Carroll uses in the poem "Jabberwocky")
> Flimps mallisify blligginocity.

The first one is not a word of English, while the second string, even if it has the appearance of being a subject-verb-object sentence, does not contain any meaningful words of English either. As evidence of the nonsensical nature of the latter, notice that if someone were to approach you and utter it in apparent seriousness, you would likely suspect that either she is speaking a language you don't know or is in need of medical intervention. Also, 'tulgey' may call up an image in your mind: perhaps if you see it as resulting from a cross between 'tug' and 'bulgy,' in which case you might visualize something large and bulbous being tugged. This, however, is not enough to make 'tulgey' a meaningful word. How do we know? Well, if someone were to use 'tulgey' in a sentence (such as 'My alpaca was incredibly tulgey'), we would have no idea what he is saying about his alpaca.[2]

CM2: Linguistic meaning is productive

Assuming that this is your first time reading this book, most of the sentences you've read in it you probably had never encountered before. And yet, so long as you are a fluent English speaker, you were able to understand these sentences with little or no effort. To do this you employed, probably unconsciously, your knowledge of the meanings of the words you read and the syntactic structure of the sentences in which they appeared, and then derived on that basis a complex meaning out of those elements. Something like this happens when you verbalize your own thoughts as well. What is more, the grammar of language spoken by human beings removes any upper limit to the complexity of sentences and phrases we can in principle understand. Just as there is no largest integer (if you think some N is the largest, just see what happens when you add 1 to it!), so too if A and B are sentences, then so are the following:

> It is not the case that A.
> Abdulla thinks that A.
> Either A is true, or B is true.
> It is quite possible that A.

What's more, each of these can then be fitted inside another to make a more complex sentence such as

> Abdulla thinks that it is quite possible that A.

This process can go on indefinitely. This in turn is due to the fact that the grammar of human languages is so constructed that it allows a potentially infinite number of sentences that count as meaningful. Granted,

---

2. We will return to qualify this point in Chapter 5, where we will consider the notion of *nonce-sense*, in which a word or phrase is used with an unprecedented meaning.

beyond, say, 250 words, a sentence will be difficult to process, and most good writers would wish to break it into its components to improve intelligibility. But any such sentence would still *be* intelligible, if only for a creature with a sufficiently powerful mind.

CM3: Words, phrases, and sentences are sometimes ambiguous

A word, phrase, or sentence may have multiple meanings. If you are told that a Parker found a bat in her car, you do not yet know whether she found a winged mammal or a sporting good in her vehicle. When a word has multiple meanings, we shall say that it is *lexically ambiguous*. This form of ambiguity is important, not least because many fallacious lines of reasoning illicitly switch between ambiguities lurking within a single word. A special type of ambiguity is *polysemy*, in which a word's multiple meanings are related to one another in a manner that is not arbitrary. For instance, if we are told that Sawyer wore a light sweater, we may not yet know whether the sweater was light in color or in weight. Yet these two kinds of "lightness" bear an affinity to one another that is not shared by the two ways of being a bat.

Philosophers have had great interest in another form of ambiguity. Consider

Every cat chased a mouse.

After a bit of reflection, you will see that this sentence might mean either

Every cat chased some mouse or other.

Or

There is some mouse that all the cats chased.

The former is the more likely interpretation, but the latter is still possible: perhaps some unfortunate mouse was ganged up on by all the cats! Similarly, consider a sentence one might encounter in debates about free will and determinism:

Every event has a cause.

This sentence could mean either

Every event has some cause or other.

Or

There is a single cause that is responsible for all events.

One can see that these two sentences mean different things by noting that the latter is "logically stronger" than the former.[3] When a phrase or sentence is ambiguous, but that ambiguity is not due to the ambiguity of any words it contains, we shall say that it is *structurally ambiguous*.

CM4: In language we may distinguish between types and tokens

A particular kind of ambiguity deserves attention before we proceed. Many nouns and noun phrases may be used to speak of a type of thing ('Dogs bark'; 'A triangle has three sides') or of particular things ('That dog has mange'; 'This triangle is equilateral.') Thus consider the question: how many words does the following sentence have?

　　1.5. Ted's dog bit another dog.

The best reply to this question is that it has not been posed carefully enough. For in one sense, (1.5) contains five words, while in another sense it contains only four words. More exactly, (1.5) contains two tokens or instances of the word 'dog,' while containing only four word types. Accordingly on the token reading of the how many words question, the answer is five, while on the type reading of that question, the answer is only four.

CM5: Words, phrases, and sentences may be either used or mentioned

We sometimes wish to draw attention to words without also using those words to make a statement or ask a question. When we do so verbally, we are mentioning those words rather than using them. We are mentioning rather than using 'throw' when we say that it is a transitive verb, or that it contains five letters, but we are using rather than mentioning the word when we say, "Throw the ball over the fence." In spoken discourse, we sometimes indicate that we are mentioning rather than using words with "finger-dance" quotes. Likewise, vocal intonation can be employed to indicate a mentioning use, as in

　　1.6. I'm not a *girl*; I'm a woman.

---

3. If A and B are propositions, A is logically stronger than B just in case A entails B but B does not entail A. We will give a definition of the notion of entailment later (p. 13).

In this book we will use either single-quotation marks to indicate mentioning uses or grant a sentence a line of its own as in (1.6) to indicate the same. Special cases of mentioning uses will be direct quotation of a real or imaginary person's utterance or thoughts; these will be indicated with double-quotation marks.

CM6: What a speaker says sometimes depends on the context in which she says it

People whose words are regularly quoted by others, such as politicians and celebrities, occasionally complain that their words were taken "out of context." Philosophers of language have been fascinated with the concept of context in recent decades, and controversy has revolved around the question of just how large a role, and what kind of role, it plays in communication. For now, we may appreciate the importance of context by noting that if each of Robin and Edison utter the sentence, "I am thirsty," there is a sense in which Robin and Edison have said the same thing, and another sense in which they've said different things. They've said the same thing in the sense that they've uttered the same series of words that do not change their meaning from one utterance to the other. But, and perhaps more importantly, they've also said different things: Robin's utterance is true only if *Robin* is thirsty, and its truth depends not at all on Edison's state of thirst. And Edison's utterance is true only if *Edison* is thirsty, and its truth does not depend at all on Robin's state of thirst. Many researchers will suggest that this difference is due to the behavior of the word 'I,' whose reference seems to depend on who is uttering it. You can construct examples to convince yourself that many other words and phrases show a similar *context sensitivity*: 'here,' 'now,' 'today,' and 'my great aunt' all seem to exhibit similar behavior. (Context sensitivity will be a topic of Chapter 5.)

CM7: In some cases, bits of language can refer to objects—even objects that do not exist

Like pictures, words have the ability to represent things—usually but not always, things distinct from themselves. Furthermore, just as a picture can represent something that doesn't exist (Kronos, the Easter Bunny, etc.), so too can a word. In fact, the two proper names I just used do exactly that. Philosophers have long been intrigued over the ability of words to represent things, including nonexistent things, and some questions that the phenomenon raises will occupy us in Chapter 2.

CM8: In certain cases, bits of language can be true, and in other cases they can be false

This may seem another point too obvious to mention, but some of the indicative sentences we use are occasionally true. Suppose I enter a room in which I see a table on which there are exactly three apples. I now remark,

> There are three apples on the table.

This sentence, as uttered in the imagined situation, would seem to be a good example of a true sentence. We will see in the next chapter that the word 'the' in this sentence harbors some subtlety that is not apparent to the naked eye (or ear), but for now let's trust our instincts on the matter. As we do so, we need not get distracted with such challenges as, How do you know that you're not being deceived by an Evil Genius into thinking that there are three apples on the table when there really are not? Instead, we are going to adopt as a working hypothesis that although we are sometimes in error in the things we say about the world, occasionally we do get things right. When this happens, it will be possible to express what we believe with a sentence that is true.

Similarly, in the situation we just imagined that involves three apples on a certain table, suppose that I had instead said,

> There are eleven apples on the table.

In that situation, I would have said something false. Let us be clear that in saying that sometimes a sentence uttered in a situation is false, we are not meaning to cast aspersions on the person making that utterance. We all make mistakes and rely on one another to correct them when possible. Of course it can be impolite to correct people's errors, and on occasion the judicious thing is to keep quiet even when you know someone else is mistaken. But even in such a situation you are probably thinking that the person is in error even if it's not worth pointing out the mistake.

We will see in later chapters that truth and falsity are central concepts for understanding linguistic meaning.

CM9: Two distinct bits of language can say the same thing

In a single language, we sometimes find words that are held by lexicographers to be synonymous. 'Furze' and 'gorse' are two English synonyms for a Scottish ground covering; 'woodchuck' and 'groundhog' are two English synonymous terms for a type of mammal. So, too, interlinguistic synonymies abound: 'Snow is white' is translated into German as 'Schnee ist weiß,' and into Catalan as 'La neu és blanca.' No doubt, some translations are difficult, and good translation of a poem or novel from one language into another is a challenging task. For our purposes, however, we need only note that some translations are also adequate. When two sentences are intertranslatable, we will say that they may be used to say the same thing. (The locution, 'What sentence S says' applies not just to indicative sentences, but to sentences of other grammatical moods as well, so that for instance it can be intelligible to ask, "What did the person in the back row who asked a question say?")

CM10: Some bits of language stand in inferential and other logical relations to other sentences

It often happens that we can infer one sentence from another. For instance, if we know that

1.7. Abdulla thinks that it is possible that A.

then we may infer that

1.8. Someone thinks that it is possible that A.

In such cases we shall say that the first sentence *entails* the second one, and we may define this notion as follows: sentence A entails sentence B if, and only if, any possible situation in which A is true is also a situation in which B is true. It sometimes happens that two sentences A and B mutually entail each other. It is tempting to conclude that in such a case, the two sentences are synonymous; that is, that they mean the same thing. We will see in Chapter 3, however, that this conclusion is controversial.

Similarly, two sentences might be *incompatible* with each other in the sense that it is not possible for both of them to be true in a single situation. For instance, (1.8) cannot be true in a situation in which the following is true:

1.9. No one thinks that it is possible that A.

For a more picturesque way of putting this, we may say that there is no possible world or situation in which both (1.8) and (1.9) are true.

CM11: Users of language often imply things in a way not captured by the relation of entailment

If a speaker states that Abdulla thinks it is possible that A, then that speaker also implies that someone thinks it is possible that A. This is due to the fact that the first sentence logically entails the second. But as speakers, we imply a variety of things that go beyond what can be captured by this entailment relation. Imagine we are working on a few different crossword puzzles, and a friend points to one that does not appear very difficult, remarking,

> Even Sydney can do this puzzle.

It is reasonable to conclude that the speaker is implying that Sydney is not the strongest crossword sleuth in the group. Similarly, a friend texts you to ask if you want to check out a new movie this evening. You reply,

> I have to study for a big test tomorrow.

In so saying, you are likely implying that you won't be able to take time out for a movie. Tone of voice, facial expression, and posture can also telegraph implications that go beyond what we say. In Chapter 4, we will look into how it is possible for a person to mean much more than she says.

1.3. Where Does Linguistic Meaning Come From?

If you have read any other literature in the Philosophy of Language before encountering this book, you may have come across the phrase 'theory of meaning.' This phrase can be puzzling to the newcomer, not least because it can be used ambiguously, sometimes, I suspect, without the writer being cognizant of that ambiguity. One disambiguation of the phrase 'theory of meaning' has to do with characterization: given that words, phrases, and sentences often have a definite meaning, how shall we describe those meanings in such a way as to accommodate and, if possible, explain some of the features of communicative meaning adduced in the last section? Candidate answers make use of such entities as propositions, concepts, truth conditions, possible worlds, or situations. Characterization questions about meaning occupy much of the field of Semantics, which is shared by Linguistics and Philosophy of Language.

A second pursuit suggested by the phrase 'theory of meaning' is to determine where meaning comes from. Given all the sounds, marks, and other configurations or perturbations of matter that occur in the world, only a small portion of them carry linguistic meaning. (The vast remainder carries natural meaning, organic meaning, or personal meaning.) What enables them to do so? We will consider the second interpretation of the "theory of meaning" question for much of the remainder of this chapter. Chapters 2 and 3 will be concerned with the "characterization" version of that question.

Iconic Theory of Meaning

The best-known answers to the question about where meaning comes from fall into three kinds: iconic theories, use theories (of which a special case is the conventionalist theory), and intentionalist theories. According to the ancient iconic theory, words have the meaning they do by virtue of perceptually resembling the things they represent. You've probably noticed that English contains a number of words that sound something like the things they're about: 'murmer,' 'splat,' and 'thrum' are examples. This phenomenon of onomatopoeia is found in a great many other human languages as well. (For instance, the Japanese word for sneezing is クシュ (pronounced like 'kushu'); 'swallow' in Hebrew is שלוק [pronounced 'shluk'].) What is more, it is natural to suppose that some nonverbal entities have the representational capacity that they do by virtue of perceptual resemblance. Perhaps a photograph manages to represent a particular thing at least in part by looking like it. Perhaps a guitar riff in a Beatles song represents weeping by sounding like a person weeping. So too, it might be suggested, perhaps words represent what they do by sounding like or in some other way perceptually resembling the things they represent.

The iconic theory of meaning has a pedigree in Western philosophy going back at least as far as Plato. In his dialogue *Cratylus*, Plato (1998) imagines (or reports—we are not certain which) a conversation among his teacher Socrates and two others, Hermogenes and Cratylus. Cratylus had been maintaining a form of Iconic Theory of Meaning, and Hermogenes turns to Socrates to help him decide whether he should be convinced. After mounting a stout defense of the theory on Cratylus' behalf, Socrates turns to debunking it. He has good reason to do so, for it faces many problems. For one, perceptual resemblance is not by itself a sufficient condition for meaning or representation. Imagine two identical twin brothers, George and Henry. Even if they happen to resemble one another a great deal along some perceptual dimension, neither represents the other. Likewise for two cars of the same make and model that have just come off an assembly line one after the other. Neither represents the other in spite of the fact that they resemble one another down to minute details.

Perceptual resemblance is not a sufficient condition for representation; nor is it a necessary condition for it. One may appreciate this most readily by considering words that represent things that are not perceptible. 'Antidisestablishmentarianism' is a term for an attitude opposing a view that attempts to undermine a close alignment of church and state. It is far from clear how such a complex position could be represented by means of something pictorial (either visually or by means of some other sensory modality), and thus unclear what it would be for this, or even any word to be perceptually similar (no matter the sensory modality) to it. 'Antidisestablishmentarianism,' then, has a definite meaning, but this meaning is not due to its being an icon of what it means.[4]

It may be tempting to reply at this point that since we do have a number of onomatopoetic words in English and other languages, perhaps the iconic theory explains how such words mean what they do, while leaving room for other explanations for other parts of language. The trouble with this suggestion is that, as we have already noted, a sound pattern's having the shape that it does is never by itself a sufficient condition for it to represent anything. Instead, the most that this sound pattern will explain is the choice on the part of speakers to use that pattern to represent something. The constellation known as the Big Dipper does not represent a ladle just by virtue of its looking very roughly the way a ladle does. Rather, this constellation represents what it does only by virtue of its being used by people to represent a ladle. But the same thing goes for words. There are plenty of sounds that we could, and sometimes do, make that are strikingly similar to sounds in the world. Consider, for instance, the sound of a coin rolling on a hard surface. Even if I happen to be talented enough to make that sound with my vocal cords, tongue, and lips, the sound I produce only represents a coin rolling on a hard surface if it is *treated* as doing so—either by me or by the community of which I am a part; otherwise it is just

---

4. When Socrates presents Cratylus with a similar objection, the latter digs in his heels and asserts that anyone who uses words that are not icons of what they represent is "banging on a brazen pot" (Plato 1998, p. 78); that is, he must therefore be speaking nonsense. This is not a compelling response, but it is a memorable image.

coincidental that the sound I make resembles that of a rolling coin. This line of thought brings us to the use theory of meaning.

Use Theory of Meaning

After providing objections such as the foregoing to the iconic theory, Socrates suggests that we will have no choice but to explain the source of linguistic meaning by appealing to "this worthless thing, convention" (Plato 1998, p. 87). Socrates does not elaborate on why he thinks appealing to convention is without value, but he may have something like the following problem in mind. According to a simple-minded view, speakers create linguistic conventions by publicly dubbing items with words that they choose for them. Imagine Adam and Eve in the Garden of Eden, and Eve takes the lead in the job of creating meanings. She points at a tree and says, "Tree!" and Adam takes note; she points at a serpent and says, "Snake!" and so on for any of the other denizens of the Garden that she cares to name. (Please see Box 1.1 for a fuller discussion of convention.)

BOX 1.1   WHAT IS A CONVENTION?

Conventions govern behavior and the products thereof, such as artifacts. There are conventional ways of speaking, dancing, and driving, as well as conventional aspects of architecture and paintings. Conventions must contain an element of the arbitrary. For instance, in certain societies it is conventional that people drive on the right side of the road; in others people drive on the left. It matters little which side people drive on so long as most drivers follow the general pattern that prevails in their society; otherwise they're liable to collide with others. By contrast, the rule that knives should have sharp blades is no convention: all else being equal, knives with sharp blades are better knives than those whose edges are blunt, whereas there is nothing inherently superior about driving on the right as opposed to driving on the left side of the road.

We have already suggested two features making up a convention: arbitrariness and regularity, in the sense that enables us to say, of a community in which there is a convention that this is "how things are done." Such regularity does not mandate universal conformity, but the practice must be widespread to a significant degree. Note, further, that the phrases 'how

continued

things are done' and 'the done thing' also convey a dimension of the normative; that is, they suggest that a certain course of action is how things are to be done. Such normativity might be ethical, but it need not be. It could instead be practical. Just as there are right and wrong ways to pedal a bicycle or brush one's teeth, so, too, there are right and wrong ways to behave, given that most others do things in a certain way. If most others drive on the right, then the prudent, and thus right, way for me is to do likewise. Similarly, if most others in a community use a certain word to name a thing, then it behooves one to do so as well in order to avoid misunderstanding. That of course does not rule out the possibility of creating a new convention, but you will need others to follow your novel practice if you are to start one.

Just because a practice is conventional, it need not be the case that all those who conform to it understand it to be. An isolated tribe of speakers who have never encountered outsiders might think that theirs is the only possible language. Apparently these speakers fail to realize that their language has arbitrary elements. Their language is still conventional in important respects even if they do not recognize it to be.

As an explanation of how words could acquire linguistic meaning, this scenario is indeed not of much value. The reason is that it presupposes what it needs to explain. For if Adam and Eve are to introduce terms for things in their environment, must they not already have a system of communication to guide their interpretation of each sound or gesture? Adam has to know how to understand Eve's pointing as an attempt to draw his attention to something, and assuming that he does, also what she is trying to get him to attend to. (Is it the apple, the apple-plus-branch, apple-plus-25 cubic feet of air surrounding it, etc.?) Further, consider for a moment the system of communication that Eve and Adam would need to share if this meaning-giving ceremony process is to be possible. Either this system is conventional, or it is not. In the former case, we are explaining conventional meaning in terms of conventional meaning, in which case we have not made much progress; in the latter case, the conventionalist view of linguistic meaning is at best incomplete and will need supplementation with some other basis for meaning. What might that other basis be?

Some philosophers have responded to this circularity problem by downplaying the role of convention in explaining linguistic meaning and emphasizing in its stead the notion of use. Ludwig Wittgenstein (1953), for instance, urges us to understand meaning through the lens of use, writing

> For a *large* class of cases—though not for all—in which we employ the word "meaning" it can be defined thus: the meaning of a word is its use in the language. (1953, §43)

Remarks such as this and others in Wittgenstein's writings are often invoked in support of a "use theory of meaning." The theory's most natural application, and likely historical impetus, is as an answer to the characterization question: instead of searching for an object that a word such as 'and' might refer to, for instance, perhaps one grasps this word's meaning by appreciating that if one has separately established both A and B, one may infer 'A and B'; further that if one has established 'A and B,' one may not only infer A but also infer B. Suppose that this strategy can generalize to other "logical" terms such as 'or' and 'not' and then beyond them to the other vocabulary as well: that may justify us in suggesting that what a word, phrase, or sentence means can be given in terms of how it is used.

The use theory could also be invoked to account for how language comes to have meaning at all: words have meaning at all by virtue of being used. This is too crude as it stands: brooms, cups, and paper clips are used but don't have meaning, at least not the sort of meaning that words have—linguistic meaning as we have termed it. On the other hand, we have already noticed that what makes a constellation in the night sky a representation of a ladle is that it is used to represent such a thing: human practices encourage stargazers to imagine seeing a ladle when gazing in a particular location in the sky. These constellations were of course found, not made, and appropriated for human purposes. By contrast, some sound patterns are produced by human beings with the aim of getting others to do certain things. For instance, count nouns (words that name objects about which it makes sense to ask, "How many are there?") such as 'rock' or 'branch,' and unlike 'snow' and 'water,' would appear to be artifacts used to get our hearers to bring types of object to mind, and perhaps also to behave in appropriate ways, such as removing a rock from our path or gathering some branches for our fire. Similarly a proper name is an artifact whose job is to get hearers to attend to an individual and perhaps also help us find or in some other way interact with it.

A communicator may aim not only to get another to attend to or think of an object but also to categorize it in a certain way, as being big, small, edible, or dangerous as the case may be. When this occurs, we begin to discern a view of language as a means of transmission of actionable information: I am aware of a situation, and it behooves me to let you know about it as well, perhaps because I want your help in responding to it. That is a good reason to tell you about it, and words are ideally suited for the task. Further, once one speaker has informed another about a situation, the other will be better equipped to act appropriately—to attack, retreat, affiliate, ingest, as the situation calls for.

We have yet to break out of the conventionalist circle, however. We may see why this is so by noting that not all uses of a word are germane to its meaning. For instance, I might use a word inappropriately—perhaps I mean 'intrepid' to mean 'insipid' for instance. Doing so does not change the English meaning of either of these words; to do that, I would at least have to get others to repeat my mistake. Supposing that this does not happen, however, we have a case in which I have used 'intrepid' incorrectly. But then it seems we need to say that only those uses that are consistent with a word's meaning are ones that count in helping to perpetuate that meaning. In that case, however, it begins to seem that the use theory is presupposing a notion of meaning—which is just the notion we have been trying to explain. Intentions might help us find a way out of this maze.

Intentional Theory of Meaning

Imagine two people who share no common language encountering one another in a wilderness. One might wish to alert the other to a danger such as the presence of a wild boar in the area. How can he do this without words? One approach would be to mimic some distinctive features of this type of animal (such as its snort and way of walking) while gazing or pointing in a certain direction. The person so behaving is doing something that perceptibly resembles some aspect of the boar. As we now know, that bit of iconicity does not by itself ensure that he will draw the other's attention to the danger. It may nevertheless enable his audience to form a reasonable hypothesis about what message he is trying to get across. Iconicity facilitates the communication of our thoughts even if it cannot stand on its own.

The individual on the receiving end in the scenario we just imagined will likely have some interpreting to do in figuring out what the speaker is getting at. Success in that enterprise likely requires imputing to the speaker an intention to convey a message about a nearby danger. The recipient of the message must therefore have a *theory of mind (ToM)*, that is, an appreciation not only that others have thoughts, but that those thoughts might be different from her own.[5] Equipped with a ToM, the recipient will have the conceptual capacity to impute to the speaker an intention to send him a message. (Otherwise, as we found in the case of Eve and Adam, he might be at a loss to discern what the other was trying to do.) The bit of iconicity the speaker's behavior contains will serve as a clue to what he is getting at.

Although this process is by no means infallible, the hearer may manage to interpret the speaker successfully. If he can do that, the two will also have set a precedent. That is, so long as they have adequate memories, and continue to engage their ToM, either one can signal boar proximity to the other on a later occasion with a probability of less interpretive effort. If, further, any others happen to be watching, they can learn the technique as well. Over time the boar-imitation skit can be stylized and abbreviated without losing its communicative value. We may also imagine similar processes resulting in the creation of an ever-growing number of noun-like expressions as well as verb-like expressions. The result might be a simple vocabulary of noun-like and verb-like behaviors that these agents could use for basic communication.[6]

The aforementioned just-so story presupposed no prior conventions. Instead, it assumes that agents have minds as well as a ToM, and that they have a modicum of rationality, some memory, and an ability to notice similarities between one person's behavior and something in her environment. One can, however, imagine out of this primordial communicative soup a system of communicative conventions coming into being. This is one reason why the Intentional Theory of Meaning captured the imagination of theorists when it was floated about a half-century ago.

The Intentional Theory of Meaning can make use of iconicity without assuming that iconicity is ever sufficient on its own to produce

---

5. See Gopnik and Wellman (1992) for discussion.

6. Linguists concerned with the historical development of language generally agree that noun-like and verb-like parts of speech were present in the earliest human languages, and that other parts of speech such as prepositions and adverbs likely came later through a process of grammaticalization, in which an expression from one part of speech gradually comes to take on a new grammatical role. See Heine and Kuteva (2007) for a detailed treatment.

linguistic meaning. Further, in light of the foregoing account of conventions in terms of regularities in behavior that have an element of arbitrariness and a dimension of normativity (see Box 1.1, "What is a Convention?"), we now have a way to overcome the circularity challenge facing traditional conventionalist theories of meaning: the boar-skit scenario we considered earlier shows how a convention can come into being where there was none before. Analogous stories may be told to help us imagine how a wide variety of words might come to have meanings among a community of speakers. As an answer to the question, in virtue of what do words have the meanings that they do, this approach has come to be known as *Intention-Based Semantics*.

Intention-Based Semantics leaves further questions unanswered. For instance, it is not clear how this theory could account for the development of words for abstract objects: if the Iconic Theory has trouble with 'antidisestablishmentarianism,' then how will the Intentional Theory do better with it? Similarly, how will the Intentional Theory make sense of how words known as "logical operators" came to have the meaning that they do? 'Or,' 'not,' and 'and,' for instance, have fairly definite meanings when they occur in sentences. 'Sergei is either on the bus or the subway' has a reasonably definite meaning that tends not to leave us puzzled as to what it is being used to say. However, we might wonder what miming or other iconic behavior could have alerted an audience to a speaker's intention to use 'or' to mean what it does. Yet if this is so, then we need to keep our eyes open for other ways in which words like this came to be imbued with meaning.

1.4. What Is Language?

So far I have been assuming that you have an intuitive familiarity with language, since you must be competent in at least one language in order to follow the text. Nonetheless, the term 'language' is sometimes used in narrow ways and at other times in very wide ways, and so it will be important to delimit the sense in which we will be using the term in what follows. To do this, we will need to define the notions of recursive syntax and compositional semantics. We say that a system of expressions has the property of being *recursive* just in case an expression of one type can occur within an expression of the same type. For instance, 'Neri' is noun, and can occur embedded within a noun phrase (NP) such as 'Neri's brother,' without violating any grammatical rules of

English.[7] Observe also that the resulting phrase can be embedded into yet another NP to yield for instance, 'Neri's brother's watch,' to yield another grammatical result, and this process can go on indefinitely.

We also need the concept of semantic compositionality, characterized as follows. Recalling our notion of linguistic meaning from earlier in this chapter, we say that a system of linguistically meaningful expressions exhibits *semantic compositionality* just in case, if any of those meaningful expressions is combined according to grammatical rules, then the resulting complex expression is meaningful, and furthermore its meaning depends in a systematic way on the meaning of its parts and their mode of combination. For instance, the sentence 'Neri saw Paolo' has a meaning that depends on the meaning of its parts (two NPs and a transitive verb), but not only that; its meaning depends on their particular manner of combination. The sentence means something different from 'Paolo saw Neri,' as you may verify by noting that one of these sentence may be true while the other is false.

With these two technical notions in place, then, we may give our definition of a language:

> *L is a language* just in case L is a system of linguistically meaningful units whose systematicity is governed by recursive syntax and compositional semantics.

This definition may appear circular, since it defines a language in terms of units that are *linguistically* meaningful. However, that circularity is apparent only, since we characterized the notion of linguistic meaning only as a matter of having stable semantic properties.

This definition of language is silent about what the units in question are: perhaps they are words, or instead morphemes,[8] or instead something even more fundamental. Likewise, the definition is neutral about the modality with which the language is used to communicate: it might be spoken, signed, written, or instead conveyed by infrared transmission. No matter. Again, for the most part we will be abstracting away from distinctions between languages such as Portuguese and Hopi, dialects of these languages, and idiolects, or versions of a language

---

7. This type of recursion is known as embedding recursion, and it is distinct from other types known as iterative recursion and succession recursion.

8. A morpheme is a word or part of a word that cannot be divided into smaller meaningful units. Thus, 'driver' is a word, but not a morpheme, since it is made up of two meaningful parts, 'drive' and the affix 'er.' Since neither of these can be divided into smaller meaningful units, however, each of them is a morpheme.

unique to an individual speaker. Bearing in mind that the concept of "Portuguese" is in a sense a huge abstraction from all the individual speakers of that language and their own idiolects, we can understand what someone means in denying that there is really such a thing as Portuguese. Nevertheless, for many purposes it can be useful to theorize at a high level of abstraction, and that is what we will try to do here.

Our definition of language does rule out more expansive notions, however. It is not difficult to find people speaking of animal languages, the language of music, the language of cinema, or even of love. At the time of the writing of this book, we do not have any compelling evidence that any nonhuman animal species has a language in the sense of that term defined here. While many nonhuman animals are able reliably to communicate information with members of their own species as well as members of others, we do not have compelling evidence of communication systems that are governed by recursive syntactic rules. That is perfectly compatible with the presence of a great many *animal communication systems* that do not conform to our definition. Likewise, musical notation has considerable structure, but it is less clear that it is governed by recursive syntax, and even if it is, not clear what the meaningful units might be that combine according to compositional principles to produce complex meanings. Similar points apply to cinema and love.

None of the foregoing is meant to denigrate animal communication, music, cinema, or love. Rather, we are adopting a narrow definition of language in order to delimit our subject matter, which is still vast even when so narrowed down. Further, if it turns out that, say, birdsong is not a language in our sense, that leaves open the possibility that it has fascinating properties that merit study on their own terms and not in a way that is prejudiced by comparison with how communication works in our own species. In addition, the fact that, to the best of current scientific knowledge, our own species is the sole possessor of language also does not show that all communication within our species is linguistic. For all the heights to which our use of language can ascend, gestures, vocal intonation, facial expression, and even pheremones may best be understood in terms of concepts that are also suitable for the understanding of animal communication.

1.5. Philosophy and Other Approaches to Language

A student new to Philosophy of Language will naturally wonder how this field differs from Linguistics. As we mentioned earlier in discussing the topic of semantics, these two fields sometimes share subject matter. However, even when this occurs, they tend to differ in emphasis. Linguists tend to take for granted certain concepts such as reference, meaning, representation, implication, and predication. This is not a shortcoming of the field, since every area of inquiry needs to take certain concepts as basic and explain other phenomena in their terms. However, philosophers welcome the opportunity to puzzle over and attempt to clarify these concepts fundamental to Linguistics. As suggested in this book's Preface, the project of puzzlement and attempted clarification is a large part of Philosophy, and so it is natural that in a book such as this we will find ourselves getting perplexed by, and then, I hope, achieving some clarity about, concepts that linguists legitimately take for granted.

Philosophy of Language tends also to abstract away from details about particular languages. A linguist might spend great effort on, for instance, constructing a grammar and lexicon for an endangered language spoken by only a few people in Amazonia. Or she might study the power of Swedish to permit the subtle construction of questions in ways surpassing many other languages. Philosophers of language value such work as this. Furthermore, their conclusions about meaning, truth, implication, reference, and the like need to be consistent with the best empirical findings from Linguistics. However, philosophers of language also tend to work at one or two steps removed from these details in order to achieve an adequately general perspective permitting theories of questions per se, rather than questions in Swedish; and of reference to past and future times per se, rather than of such references in Yoruba. But being abstract is not the same thing as being a priori, or knowable without recourse to empirical investigation: as we have noted, and as you will see in more detail in later chapters, positions in the Philosophy of Language need to hold up under the light shed by empirical linguistic inquiry. Not all such positions survive the scrutiny.

1.6. Study Questions and Suggestions for Further Reading

Study Questions

1. Please review the distinction between lexical and structural ambiguity. In light of that, can a sentence or phrase be structurally ambiguous without containing any lexical ambiguity? Please explain your answer. Next, consider the sentence 'The ranger saw the hiker with binoculars.' Is this sentence ambiguous? If so, please show how it is and explain the type of ambiguity it exhibits.

2. Describe an example in which a speaker implies something that goes beyond the literal meaning of her words. How might a listener discern that added layer of meaning?

3. After reviewing the definition of 'entailment,' please formulate a case of two distinct sentences that entail each other. Please try to show that they do in fact in fact entail each other.

4. Suppose that after carefully observing some nonhuman animals you feel confident that they are communicating in some way, even if they are not using language in the sense of that term defined in this chapter. How might you go about establishing that these animals are indeed communicating?

5. Keeping in mind both the use/mention and the type/token distinctions, consider the following sentence: 'Salia has five letters.' Suppose further that Salia has just retrieved five letters from her mailbox. Please explain how the italicized sentence has three disambiguations, on two of which it is true, and on another of which it is false. (Add single-quotation marks where appropriate.)

Further Reading (with recommended [*] items for instructors)

The classic discussion of a distinction between natural and speaker meaning is in Grice ([1957] 1989).* Schiffer (1973) elucidates Grice's approach while also elaborating and defending Intention-Based Semantics. Lewis (1969) uses the tools of classical two-person game theory to show how conventions, including linguistic conventions, can arise in the absence of any prior conventions. Anderson (2006) offers a challenging critique of views ascribing language proper to nonhuman animals. Charlesworth and Charlesworth (2017) provide a brief and accessible introduction to the essential ideas of evolution through natural selection. Everett (2012) presents intriguing arguments against the view that human natural language is necessarily recursive. Fitch (2010) is a wide-ranging survey of research on language evolution. Marler and Slabberkoorn (2004) is a monumental treatment of birdsong and bird calls. Davies (1994) contains a careful discussion of the idea that music might be construed as a language. Darwin's classic work on emotions and their expression is Darwin ([1872] 1998), and this volume has been carefully annotated by the psychologist P. Ekman with reference to recent studies on topics that Darwin discusses. Gopnik and Wellman (1992) is a helpful discussion of the concept of theory of mind. Szabo (2017) provides motivation and a clear account of the concept of semantic compositionality, and considers some challenges to the claim that it accurately describes natural languages. Green (2007) explains the notion of organic meaning and distinguishes it from both natural and speaker meaning. Green (2007) also discusses research on the evolution and communicative function of human facial expressions. Plato's *Cratylus** is a readable and at times humorous dialogue revealing the temptations and limitations of iconicity in explaining meaning. Rousseau (2017) offers a conjecture on the origin of language based on its role in the expression of emotion. A broad overview of the history of Philosophy of Language covering over two millennia may be found in Cameron et al. (2017).

References

Anderson, S. 2006. *Dr. Dolittle's Delusion: Animals and the Ununiqueness of Human Language*. New Haven, CT: Yale University Press.

Cameron, M., Hill, B., and Stainton, R. 2017. *Sourcebook in the History of the Philosophy of Language: Primary Texts from the Pro-Socratics to Mill*. Berlin, Germany: Springer.

Charlesworth, B., and Charlesworth, D. 2017. *Evolution: A Very Short Introduction*. Oxford: Oxford University Press.

Darwin, C. (1872) 1998. *The Expression of the Emotions in Man and Animals*. 3rd ed. Edited by P. Ekman. New York: Oxford University Press

Davies, S. 1994. *Musical Meaning and Expression*. Ithaca, NY: Cornell University Press.

Everett, D. 2012. "What Does Pirahã Grammar Have to Teach Us about the Human Mind?" *WIREs Cognitive Science* 3: 555–563.

Fitch, T. 2010. *The Evolution of Language*. Oxford: Oxford University Press.

Gopnik, A., and Wellman, H. 1992. "Why the Child's Theory of Mind Really is a Theory." *Mind and Language* 7: 145–171.

Green, M. 2007. *Self-Expression*. Oxford: Oxford University Press.

Grice, H. 1957. "Meaning." *Philosophical Review*. Reprinted in his *Studies in the Way of Words*. Cambridge, MA: Harvard University Press.

Heine, B., and Kuteva, T. 2007. *The Genesis of Grammar: A Reconstruction*. New York: Oxford University Press.

Keltner, D., Ekman, P., Gonzaga, G., and Beer, J. 2003. "Facial Expression of Emotion." In *Handbook of Affective Sciences*, edited by Richard J. Davidson, Klaus R. Scherer, and H. Hill Goldsmith, 415–432. New York: Oxford University Press.

Lewis, D. (1969) 2002. *Convention: A Philosophical Study*. Oxford: Blackwell.

Marek, P., Papaj, D., Yeager, J., Milina, S., and Moore, W. 2011. "Bioluminescent Aposematism in Millipedes." *Current Biology* 21: R6809–R6810.

Marler, P., and Slabberkoorn, H. 2004. *Nature's Music: The Science of Birdsong*. London: Elsevier.

Plato. 1998. *Cratylus*. Translated by C. D. C. Reeve. Indianapolis, IN: Hackett.

Rousseau, J. J. 2017. *Essay on the Origin of Language*. In Cameron et al., 887–909.

Schiffer, S. 1973. *Meaning*. Oxford: Oxford University Press.

Szabo, Z. 2017. "Compositionality." In *The Stanford Encyclopedia of Philosophy*, edited by Edward N. Zalta. https://plato.stanford.edu/

Wittgenstein, L. 1953. *Philosophical Investigations*. Translated by G. E. M. Anscombe. Oxford: Blackwell.

CHAPTER 2

Characterizing Linguistic Meaning

Chapter Overview

So far we have primarily considered the in-virtue-of-what question in order to make headway on the source of linguistic meaning. For this and the next chapter, our focus will be on the characterization question: assuming that words, phrases, and sentences have meaning, how shall we characterize the way or ways in which they do so? We first consider some initially attractive answers to this question that appeal to dictionary definitions, ideas, verification conditions, and conditions of usage, as well as the Ordinary Language movement that the usage theory spawned. Discerning the limitations of the Ordinary Language movement will enable us to articulate a respect in which linguistic meaning is autonomous from occasions of use.

2.1. Constraints on Characterizations

When we ask the characterization question, we are looking for ways to characterize the meanings of words, phrases, and the larger chunks of language built from them, such as sentences, with the aim of accounting for the eleven desiderata mentioned in the previous chapter. For instance, we wish to characterize meaning in such a way as to accommodate and, if possible, make sense of the fact that component meanings combine in systematic ways to produce complex meanings—what we have called semantic compositionality. We have already noted, under CM2 of the previous chapter, that language is productive. We are now able to formulate a more specific aspect of the productivity of language. For instance, consider the difference between an ordered pair <a, b> and a set that contains those same two members {a, b}. In sets, order makes no difference, so that {a, b} = {b, a}. The same is not true of series such as ordered pairs: <a, b> ≠ <b, a>. It is widely agreed among students of language that complex linguistic items such as phrases, clauses, and sentences are more like ordered n-tuples (where n can be any integer) than they are like sets. This is mirrored by the fact that a sentence, for instance, is not a list of words: in a list, such as the things I need at the hardware store, order does not matter. However, in a sentence, order normally matters a great deal. Consider the difference in meaning between these two sentences:

> 2.1.   Merckx beat Gimondi.
> Gimondi beat Merckx.

For millions of cycling fans, which one of these sentences was true and which false was a matter of utmost importance in the 1973 Giro d'Italia. That, however, would make little sense if a sentence were a list of words, since these two sentences contain precisely the same ones. Although not all aspects of word order in a sentence make a difference for what it means,[1] in many important cases word order does matter. As a result, if we are to have a comprehensive approach to characterizing meaning, we need to think of sentences as being structured at least up to the point of being ordered. We may capture the general point here with the thought that the semantic value of a complex linguistic expression depends in a systematic way on the semantic values of its component elements together with the way in which they are combined.

'Depends on' in the earlier formulation hides a subtlety, however. It might either mean 'depends in part on,' or it might mean 'depends on, and only on.' The latter construal leads to a strong formulation of semantic compositionality according to which the semantic value of a complex expression is a *function* of the semantic values of its components and their mode of composition: the definition of a function requires that the semantic value of the input uniquely determines the semantic value of the output. By contrast, the former, 'depends in part on,' construal leads to a weaker formulation on which that input might in principle interact

---

1. For instance, the two sentences "I picked up the keys" and "I picked the keys up" mean the same thing despite their difference, at least at a superficial level, in word order.

with other factors to determine the semantic value of the output. So long as that determination process is sufficiently systematic to enable speakers reliably to comprehend complex expressions, this weaker version of semantic compositionality may be adequate to account for the facts of language production and comprehension. Accordingly, we may distinguish between two theses:

> *Weak Semantic Compositionality*: The semantic value of a complex expression depends at least in part on the semantic values of its components and their mode of composition.
>
> *Strong Semantic Compositionality*: The semantic value of a complex expression depends on the semantic value of its components and their mode of composition, and upon nothing else.

In Chapter 4 we will encounter some reasons for preferring Weak Semantic Compositionality over its Strong counterpart. For now, let us observe that Weak Compositionality is compatible with complex linguistic meanings being built up in a systematic way. That may in turn be enough to explain how speakers are able to comprehend nearly effortlessly sentences they have never encountered before.

Aside from respecting its compositional features, we may also wish to characterize meaning in such a way as to accommodate and, if possible, make sense of the fact that some sentences stand in logical relations to one another (CM10). From the premise that most dogs have tails, we may infer that some dogs have tails. Likewise, from the premises that Mary is friends with Susan, and that Susan is the same person as Ms. Thomas, we may infer that Mary is friends with Ms. Thomas (even if, not knowing her last name, Mary is unaware of this fact). Answers to the characterization question should if possible make sense of these phenomena. It would in fact be further validation of a particular semantic characterization if it could help us solve a problem such as that posed by a puzzling line of reasoning, one of which we'll encounter in the next chapter. If a semantic characterization can shed light on whether that line of reasoning is persuasive or instead harbors a subtle sleight of hand, that will be evidence in that characterization's favor.

2.2. Dictionaries

A few possible answers to this characterization question may come readily to mind for many readers. For instance, it may seem obvious that the way to characterize a word's meaning is by picking up a dictionary and checking its definition. Thus we find that the *Merriam-Webster's Dictionary* defines 'oblate' as an adjective meaning 'flattened or depressed at the poles.' If you don't know what this word means, that definition would help so long as you know the meanings of the words used to define it ('flattened,' 'poles,' etc.); it is also helpful to learn that the word is an adjective rather than a preposition or a verb. On the other hand, we may still wonder how to characterize the meanings of the words used to define 'oblate.' We could of course go back to the dictionary to define them, but doing so will launch us on an endless task if we do not already know the meanings of the words we're using to define the ones we started with. Further, the dictionary definition approach does not tell us how this word contributes its meaning to the sentences in which it occurs. That is, the dictionary approach does not bear out the realization that sentences are not mere lists of words. Similarly, the dictionary approach will not explain why one sentence might stand in a logical relation to another, or why two sentences might be incompatible, in the sense of being such that not both can be true simultaneously. For instance, the dictionary definition will not tell us whether it is possible for an object to be both oblate and prolate. For these reasons, checking in dictionaries might be a useful first step in characterizing meaning, but it leaves the hard questions untouched.

2.3. Ideas

Another thought comes naturally as a strategy for characterizing meaning: perhaps the meaning of the word 'dog' may be characterized by its association with my idea of a dog; and perhaps even the meaning of 'antidisestablishmentarianism' may be explained by its association with the idea of a particular doctrine concerning the relation of church to state. To get a better grip on the line of thought here, let's observe that I may acquire ideas through experience, although nothing in principle rules out the possibility of some of those ideas being innate.[2] I am pretty sure

---

2. The English philosopher John Locke (1632–1704) is well known for drawing from his empiricist premises the conclusion that there can be no innate ideas. However, modern-day empiricists need not follow him in this. If empiricism is the view that all knowledge comes from, and comes only from, sensory experience, it does not follow from this doctrine that all knowledge comes from, and only from, the sensory experience that an organism has during its lifetime. Instead, it is at least possible in principle that some knowledge derives from experience had by an organism's ancestors and is passed down through genetic inheritance.

I was born without an idea of a carburetor, or of depreciation, but rather acquired them with experience of automobiles and financial matters, respectively. On the assumption that the word 'carburetor' was given its meaning by being attached to that idea of a carburetor, perhaps we could also hold that its meaning should be explained in terms of that idea.

This suggestion is sometimes termed the *ideational theory of meaning*. It is a theory most closely associated with John Locke, who devotes the third of the four books comprising his *Essay Concerning Human Understanding* (1690) to language. Early in Book III, Locke writes,

> Words in their primary or immediate Signification, stand for nothing, but the ideas in the mind of him that uses them. (1690, Bk. III, sec. 2)

Many students new to the Philosophy of Language find an ideational view like Locke's attractive. For one, given CM6 mentioned in Chapter 1, even if Kronos does not exist, my idea of him seems to do so. And so if my name for Kronos refers to my idea, then that name will still have something to refer to even if that deity does not exist. Likewise, two names for the same thing, like 'Mark Twain' and 'Sam Clemens,' appear to differ in meaning, even though they refer to the same individual. If so, that might be explained in terms of the fact that the ideas I associate with each name are different: 'Mark Twain' I associate with the idea of a man with a handlebar moustache who played a lot of billiards and wrote famous coming-of-age novels. 'Sam Clemens' I associate with the idea of a riverboat captain on the Mississippi.

The ideational theory, then, is initially appealing, but it faces a serious objection. For the contention that our words regularly refer to our ideas does not on closer inspection square with common sense. When I say, or think to myself, that my coffee is cold, I seem to be referring to the coffee and not to my idea of the coffee. After all, what sense can we make of an idea of mine literally being cold? John Stuart Mill put the point forcefully, writing,

> When I say, "the sun is the cause of day," I do not mean that my idea of the sun causes or excites in me the idea of day; or in other words, that thinking of the sun makes me think of day. I mean, that a certain physical fact, which is called the sun's presence ... causes another physical fact, which is called day. (Mill 1882, chap. 2)

The ideational theory seems to imply that when we mean to be speaking about things in the world, we always end up speaking of aspects of ourselves, namely our ideas. Of course, we do sometimes want to mention our own ideas, such as when I say, "Then I came up with the idea of cutting open the coconut with a chainsaw!" But later, when we do wish to discuss things that are not ideas, the ideational theory can make no sense of how this is possible.

Please glance back at the remark of Locke's quoted earlier. He states that in their primary or immediate signification, words stand only for ideas. Does that way of putting matters leave room for the possibility that names have secondary or mediate signification that is different, perhaps for instance a reference to things in the world that our ideas represent? In fact, Locke ambivalently suggests as much later in Book III of the *Essay*, where he remarks that people attempt in their uses of words to refer to two other things besides their own ideas. First, they try to make their ideas refer to the ideas of other people, presumably in order to make communication more successful. Second, people attempt in their use of words to make a "secret reference" to things in the world that their ideas represent (Bk III, chap. 2, §4). But then soon after that, Locke tells us that it is a "perversion" of language to attempt to make words refer to anything but our ideas! (Bk III, chap. 2, §5)

Locke seems to have had an inkling of difficulties with the ideational theory without knowing how to resolve them. Further, he was rightly sensitive to the way in which many words do not seem to be in the business of referring to or naming things. Particularly if we are in the empiricist tradition as Locke was, we will tend to associate ideas with images: it would be natural to think that I have an idea of a bighorn sheep at least in part because I can form a mental picture of that type of animal. However, even if that mental picture explains how it is possible for me to have an idea of such a creature (and even this is a controversial position), there seem to be plenty of phenomena of which it is hard to see how a mental picture is even possible. Return to our example of antidisestablishmentarianism. What could a mental picture of that possibly be? A similar problem arises for myriad other abstract concepts such as justice, erudition, or genetic drift. Second, even if we had a mental picture associated with a concept, it is not clear what such a picture would explain. Consider a sentence such as 'Either frogs croak or dogs bark.' It says something different from the sentence 'Frogs croak and dogs bark' and from the sentence 'Most frogs croak.' Further, that difference seems to be accounted for by the different meanings of 'or,' 'and,' and 'most.' Even if we had a mental picture associated with 'or,' it is obscure how it could explain such facts as that we know that a sentence having the form 'A or B' is true if and only if either 'A' is true or 'B' is true; that a sentence of the form 'A or B' is implied by the truth of 'A' and implied by the truth of 'B,' and so on. Likewise, one might suggest that the meaning of 'establishmentarianism' can be captured by a picture of a church drawn next to a government building which is itself drawn with human-like features looking at it approvingly; then 'disestablish-mentarianism' could perhaps be captured by putting a red circle with an X mark across this last picture; and then the 'anti' will be achieved by a further red cross with red X superimposed on the first one. Phew! Complicated. But the complexity is not the problem. The problem is that this explanation makes use of things that are not strictly pictorial in order to capture or characterize a word's meaning. For instance, the red circle with X inside is a conventional symbol meaning that the entity depicted inside the circle is to be avoided or rejected. But now we are explaining how one idea means what it does by appealing to how another one means what *it* does; moreover, the latter idea has whatever significance it has by being subject to a convention of a certain kind: red circles with crosses through them mean that the things inside of them are bad or otherwise to be avoided. Ideas-as-images are now being explained in terms of conventions and not just their pictorial quality.

A number of themes emerge from these reflections. First, when we are attempting to make progress on the characterization question about meaning, it appears to be a methodological mistake to consider words in isolation from the sentences in which they occur. Stare as long as you wish at the word 'or,' and you will, I predict, be unable to discern its meaning in isolation. Instead, you need to discern what that word does to the sentences in which it occurs.

Second, imagery is at best only partially helpful in the characterization of meaning. Even if a person associates an image with a word or phrase, she needs to use that image in the right way in order to know how to use that bit of language. Further, there are plenty of meaningful bits of language that do not seem to associate in any interesting or useful way with imagery.

Particularly given their association with imagery, ideas do not seem well suited as tools to help with characterizing meaning. However, please recall our recent example of a carburetor. Many people know that this is a device for mixing fuel and air for internal combustion engines. Yet only a portion of those people know what carburetors looks like.

It is popular nowadays to say that those of us who lack any mental image of a carburetor still have a *concept* of such things. As a result of being detached from mental images, might concepts be a more flexible tool for elucidating meaning than are ideas? We will take a step toward answering that question by considering a view of meaning tied to the notion of verification.

2.4. Verification Conditions

Certain approaches to characterization also have a polemical side. For instance, by the latter part of the nineteenth century, some philosophers were tending to write in such a way as to leave readers with the sneaking suspicion that the reason their writings were so hard to understand was that they were speaking nonsense, albeit a subtle and sophisticated form of nonsense. For instance, the British Idealist philosopher F. H. Bradley (1846–1924) once tried to explain his concept of a "finite center" as follows:

> a finite center, when we speak strictly, is not itself in time. It is an immediate experience of itself and of the Universe in one. It comes to itself as all the world and not as one world among others. And it has properly no duration through which it lasts. ... A finite center may indeed be called duration in the sense of presence. But such a present is not any time which is opposed to a past and future. It is temporal in the sense of being itself the positive and concrete negation of time. (Bradley 1994, pp. 326–327)

Like much other philosophical writing that was influential in the late nineteenth and early twentieth centuries, this passage is esoteric to say the least. But unlike esoteric writing we might encounter in chemistry or biology, we may be at a loss to know what possible empirical tests could be performed that might help us tell whether what Bradley says is correct or not. Are there any instruments that could detect finite centers, or do they leave traces of themselves that although minute are still detectable by the unaided senses?

In the period between World Wars I and II, a new philosophical movement developed that was inspired in part by recent developments in logic (of which more in a moment) as well as the natural sciences. This movement came to be known either as Logical Positivism or Logical Empiricism (I will use the latter term), and it counted both scientists and philosophers among its members. Logical Empiricists took inspiration from some strongly worded remarks of David Hume written some 150 years earlier:

> If we take in our hand any volume; of divinity, or school metaphysics, for instance; let us ask, *Does it contain any abstract reasoning concerning quantity or number?* No. *Does it contain any experimental reasoning concerning matter of fact and existence?* No. Commit it then to the flames. For it can contain nothing but sophistry and illusion. (Hume 1777, p. 165; italics original)

In a like spirit of reforming philosophical and other types of discourse, Logical Empiricists suggested a characterization of meaning in terms of the possibility of verification or falsification by empirical means—be they our unaided senses, or instruments built to enhance them such as microscopes, radio telescopes, cloud chambers, or particle accelerators. On the Logical Empiricist approach, a sentence should be counted as cognitively meaningful only if we have some idea how to use empirical means to confirm or disconfirm it.[3] That would include not just our unaided senses but also instruments such as those mentioned earlier. It would, however, exclude consulting an allegedly holy text, an astrologer, or an oracle such as the ancient Greeks believed to reside at the Temple of Delphi. The reason for this exclusion is that although we have to use our senses to, for example, read the holy text, we apparently have no way of empirically determining its holiness, that is, of empirically determining that it represents the words of a divine being.

The Logical Empiricists were well aware that we take many statements to be true by definition. A closely related notion is that of *analytic truth*, or truth that holds by virtue of meaning alone. The claims that triangles are three-sided, that Tuesday follows Monday, and that physical objects take up some region of space-time, might be thought to be knowable just by analyzing the concepts of triangle, Monday, Tuesday, and physical object, respectively. For this reason, each of these three sentences might be considered an analytic truth. By contrast, a *synthetic truth* is any true sentence that is not analytic. It seems to follow that a synthetic truth, if it is knowable, will only be known by appeal to experience. (Examples might include 'The liquid in the beaker turned blue' or 'Galaxy 458-H is rotating.')

---

3. We will return shortly to explain the use of the qualifier "cognitive" by contrasting it with the notion of emotive meaning.

The Logical Empiricists held that analytic sentences are meaningful but are so only by virtue of serving to codify our definitions. They held the same view of the truths of mathematics: '2 + 2 = 4' is true by virtue of the meanings of the symbols that that sentence contains. By contrast, other sentences, if they purport to describe the world—the so-called synthetic sentences—had better pass muster with a standard of empirical testability. That standard is associated with two complementary principles:

> **LE1.** A sentence is cognitively meaningful if and only if it is either analytic, or there is some way to either confirm or disconfirm it by empirical means.

> **LE2.** A nonanalytic sentence's cognitive meaning, if it has any, is its conditions of confirmation or disconfirmation.

Neither LE1 nor LE2 entails the other. However, the two principles go naturally together, and LE2 is only worth propounding if we are convinced of LE1. So let us reflect on LE1. As suggested by our quotation from Bradley, his readers will at least be challenged to show that his claims pass that test; so too for other philosophers of his era and many others who have come since. As Hume suggests, entire books of metaphysics, epistemology, and the like will be deemed devoid of cognitive significance, and their writers will have been under the illusion of making sense! As another illustration, consider radical skepticism, according to which we have no way of ruling out the possibility that we are living in a Matrix-like world in which we spend our days inside pods generating electricity for malevolent machines. (After all, any experience you could have that seems to rule out that hypothesis might just have been synthesized by those machines to allay your fears.) According to LE1, debating whether that skeptical possibility is realized or not will inevitably use language that is cognitively insignificant. The reason is that no possible empirical test could settle whether or not the Matrix scenario is true. Any evidence that we think might vindicate that scenario would equally support the commonsense view that we live in a non-Matrix world. Therefore, concludes the Logical Empiricist, debates over the relative merits of such radical skepticism or the commonsense view are, strictly speaking, nonsense.

Or consider ethical statements. We often make claims about what is right or wrong: most of us will agree that publicly humiliating a person in order to get pleasure out of her discomfort is immoral. But here again it is difficult to see what empirical tests we might carry out to establish, or for that matter falsify, this claim. One might suggest that we do a test to see whether someone publicly humiliated experiences increased stress levels, heightened inflammation, or subsequent difficulty sleeping. However, even if we found all these consequences to flow from a person's being publicly humiliated, that would not show that it is *morally* wrong to put her in such a situation. After all, there are plenty of other situations that produce similar results (starting a new job, taking a high-stakes standardized test, undergoing a painful dental procedure) that we would not consider to be morally wrong. More would have to be done to show that public humiliation is immoral. In addition to ethical discourse, one readily supposes that similar objections arise for sentences that are part of religious discourse ('God is omnipresent'), as well as sentences that are used in aesthetic discourse ('That sonata is melancholy'). (We will see in a moment that the Logical Empiricist holds that ethical, theological, and aesthetic discourse may have a noncognitive kind of meaning.)

We might also point out that a good portion of language is not apt for empirical decidability as a result of not being used to describe anything. Asking how empirically to verify or falsify a sentence in the imperative mood, such as 'Shut the door,' just seems to be misplaced. Likewise for an interrogative sentence such as 'Where is Arianna?' The Logical Empiricist could, however, resist the temptation to relegate all interrogatives to the realm of the cognitively insignificant. Aristotle said that philosophy begins in wonder, and we could acknowledge this insight by supposing that an interrogative is cognitively significant so long as we have some conceivable empirical means of *answering* it.

The Logical Empiricists threw bracingly cold water on some problematic trends in philosophical thought; they also generally held themselves to high standards of clarity in their own writings. However, their severe strictures on meaningfulness faced great obstacles. For one, their doctrine of mathematics as a branch of logic, and thus as analytic (a view which came to be known as logicism), ran into severe technical problems in light of K. Gödel's proofs of the incompleteness of arithmetic: no consistent logical system will be adequate to prove all the results of arithmetic, itself needed to deduce large swaths of mathematics.[4] Further, as W. V. Quine (1951) argued, it's awfully hard

---

4. Smith (2007) gives an accessible account of Godel's results and their philosophical significance.

to find a satisfying delineation between analytic and synthetic sentences. Take our earlier example of physical objects occupying regions of space-time: if our most sophisticated and successful physics ended up denying this claim by positing physical objects taking up no more space-time than a mathematical point, it would be rash to reject such a theory out of hand. Finally, consider LE1 itself: what empirical tests might one perform to establish *it*? Surely just tallying up a bunch of sentences that can be empirically confirmed or disconfirmed will not be enough to do so, since that will leave open the question whether those sentences that are not empirically decidable are meaningful or not. At the same time, it does not seem that LE1 should count as an analytic truth. This raises what is known as the *self-application problem* for Logical Empiricism: LE1 does not seem to be either analytically true or empirically decidable, whence it is not cognitively meaningful by its own standards.

Another objection to LE1 was raised by I. Berlin (1939), who asks: in order to put a sentence up to the test of empirical confirmation or disconfirmation, don't I already have to know what it means? But if so, then LE1 would seem to be useless in delimiting the cognitively significant sentences from the rest. However, the Logical Empiricist should be able to answer this question. One way to find such an answer takes its cue from the phenomenon of *illusions of meaning*, that is, cases of sentences that seem to make sense, but that on closer inspection do not do so. Examples follow:

2.1. More people have been to Greenland than I have.
2.2. The blue house on the corner is very unique.
2.3. Can a man marry his widow's sister?

Close inspection will reveal that none of these sentences makes sense. Each one seems to mean something but, in fact, does not. In the case of 2.2, with LE1 in hand we might be tempted to head over to the blue house on the corner (assuming that we know which one the speaker is referring to) to begin to inspect what is unique about it. However, once we reflect on the concept of uniqueness, we realize that 'unique' means 'being the only one of its kind,' and that this characteristic does not come in degrees. It therefore makes no sense to call anything 'very unique.' We may for this reason conclude that no possible experience could confirm or disconfirm 2.2. It is thus bereft of cognitive significance and ready to be cast into your fireplace. However, the words in 2.2 gave you some clue as to how to confirm or disconfirm it empirically, even if the task turned out to be a fool's errand. But then, given this phenomenon of illusions of meaning, cannot the Logical Empiricist point out in response to Berlin that many sentences carry with them a *seeming* meaningfulness, which should be enough to give us clues as to how to go about confirming it or disconfirming them by empirical means.

We said that that there would be little point in espousing LE2 if one does not also espouse LE1. Given the difficulties we just encountered with the latter, I will pass over difficulties with the former. Instead, it will be more expedient for us to consider what Logical Empiricists had to say about normative discourse,[5] as their position on this issue continues to reverberate to this day. After denying that it possesses cognitive significance, A. J. Ayer (1936) developed an ingenious strategy for saving normative discourse from the realm of nonsense. To this end, he argues that normative discourse does not set out to make statements about the world; rather, its aim is instead to express approval or disapproval and in some cases to exhort others to action as well. Discussing ethical language, which is a prominent case of normative discourse, Ayer writes:

> The presence of an ethical symbol in a proposition adds nothing to its factual content. Thus if I say to someone, "You acted wrongly in stealing that money," I am not stating anything more than if I had simply said, "You stole that money." In adding that this action is wrong I am not making a further statement about it. I am simply evincing my moral disapproval of it. (Ayer 1936, p. 107)

For Ayer, ethical discourse has "emotive" meaning even if it lacks cognitive meaning. He also holds that in using ethical language to express approval or disapproval, speakers normally aim to arouse feelings in others and to stimulate them to action or to the avoidance of certain actions (p. 108). He sums up his observations as follows:

> In fact we may define the meaning of the various ethical words in terms of the different feelings they are normally taken to express, and also the different responses which they are calculated to provoke. (Ayer 1936, p. 108)

---

5. Normative discourse is discourse about what someone should do. As such, it includes discourse about ethical norms ("Don't lie"), practical norms ("Hydrate frequently when exercising in hot weather"), and norms of etiquette ("Eat with your mouth closed"), among others.

We will see below that this "emotivist" claim about the meaning of ethical words must confront a strong objection. Until then, however, let us observe that Ayer and many whom he inspired have tended to take the notion of expression as an unexplained primitive, elucidating it only by contrast with other types of language use such as assertion. Similarly, another prominent Logical Empiricist, Rudolph Carnap, says the following in a brief remark distinguishing expression from assertion:

> The laughter does not assert the merry mood but *expresses* it. It is neither true nor false because it does not assert anything, although it may be either genuine or deceptive. (Canap 1935, p. 28)

Any theoretical enterprise must take some notion(s) as primitive, so taking expression as primitive is not itself objectionable. We will, however, pave the way for later discussion by shedding some light on this notion. First of all, what we express are states of mind, such as approval, disapproval, indifference, contempt, and enthusiasm. We express emotions such as happiness, sadness, disgust, and anger, as well as cognitive states such as beliefs and so-called conative states such as intentions. Further, as Carnap notes, behavior that expresses states of mind need not involve stating or asserting that one is in such a state: I can express my anger by scowling, yelling, or throwing furniture across the room, but in so doing I am not stating that I am angry.[6]

In suggesting that expressions of emotion, belief, or intention may be genuine or deceptive, Carnap is also indicating that a mere manifestation of a psychological state is not as such an expression of that state. My running away from a dangerous animal is a manifestation of fear, but not an expression of fear; likewise for my increased heartrate and galvanic skin response in that situation.

What is the difference between manifesting a state of mind and expressing that state? One proposal has it that we move from manifestation to expression with behavior or a trait that is designed to convey information about the manifested psychological state. Recall from our discussion in Chapter 1 that a process or object can be designed to do a certain job even if it was not crafted by an intelligent designer for that job. In that light, we may note that even an involuntary facial expression

---

6. We also use the notion of expression in saying for instance that a sentence expresses a proposition. This usage likely derives from the usage of 'express' to capture the phenomenon of manifesting our states of mind.

or behavior such as laughter may be designed to convey information about its owner's affective state. In this case, the most likely designer is evolution through natural selection—a process entirely lacking in intentions, plans, or goals. A facial expression or other behavior might be intentionally produced for the purpose of conveying information, but it need not be in order to count as expressive behavior.

It also helps to distinguish between expressing one's psychological state and expressive language. The latter might be used to express one's psychological state but need not do so. Thus if the emotivist approach to ethical discourse is correct, we may see 'x is wrong' as a device whose job is to express disapproval of a certain type of action; which type depends on what noun or noun phrase goes to fill in the 'x.' However, just as one can whistle a happy tune without being happy, so too, a speaker might use a sentence such as 'Stealing is wrong,' without being sincere; in this case she is using an expressive device without expressing her own viewpoint. This distinction will prove useful again when we discuss speech acts in Chapter 5 and slurs in Chapter 7.

2.5. Usage, Emotivism, and the Autonomy of Meaning

One appealing aspect of the doctrine of meaning as use is that it suggests an answer both to the in-virtue-of-what question and to the characterization questions about the nature of meaning. However, we saw in the last chapter that the former answer needs refinement if it is to become plausible: otherwise, all aspects of how a word or expression is used will turn out to be features of its meaning. A similar challenge faces attempts to apply the doctrine to the characterization question. The reason is as follows. How a word, phrase, or expression is used may not bear directly on its meaning. For instance, in everyday English, we commonly use the phrase 'spring chicken' to refer only to those who are elderly (as in "She's no spring chicken!," said of a nonagenarian). This fact would, according to the meaning-as-use theory, seem to imply that part of the meaning of 'spring chicken' is that it refers to the elderly. However, it is well within the literal meaning of that phrase to point to a two-year-old child and say, "Now *that* is a spring chicken!" After all, what could possibly be a better example of a spring chicken than that child? This is in spite of the fact that we rarely use 'spring chicken' to refer to small children. From this example it would seem to follow that there is no straightforward way to read off meaning from use. We might of course respond to this challenge by noting that we should only consider those aspects of use that are mandated or permitted by a term's or expression's meaning. However, in so doing we would be explaining meaning in terms of meaning—which would not be terribly illuminating.

Proponents of the doctrine of meaning as use tended to distance themselves from the Logical Empiricists' rigorous constraints on cognitive significance in language. However, many of them retained sympathy with the emotivist approach to ethical discourse or some variant thereof. They also carried a torch for the idea that some traditional philosophical questions are best treated not by being solved but by being *dissolved*. As we will see in Chapter 3, Bertrand Russell's approach to description-containing sentences was considered a paradigm of this kind of strategy. The Logical Empiricists adopted a similar strategy in arguing that many traditional philosophical questions are bereft of cognitive significance. By the middle of the twentieth century, the idea of meaning as use had developed into what we now call the Ordinary Language movement, according to which many traditional problems of philosophy cannot even be posed without committing a misuse of language, even if that misuse is a subtle one.

Here is an example of the Ordinary Language strategy in action. The traditional problem of freedom of will asks, given that we live in a largely causally deterministic universe, how can human actions ever be counted as free? After all, even a banal act such as scratching my own left earlobe is the result of a deterministic causal process running from my central nervous system, through my muscles, and ending up in movements of my arm and finger. But my central nervous system is also a mere hunk of matter governed by causal laws, and its own activities are themselves results of deterministic processes traceable to others outside it. How, then, can we justifiably take ourselves to perform banal actions freely; further, if those are unfree, then the prospects of more sophisticated acts like playing a sonata or a game of soccer being free would seem dim indeed.

The Ordinary Language philosopher will reply by suggesting that the aforementioned is a mere pseudo-problem that can only be formulated by abusing ordinary language. The reason, she will aver, is that we normally speak of free or unfree actions in situations in which some moral or legal issue has been raised—for instance, when a person has been accused of a crime. By contrast, imagine you observe someone sitting alone on a park bench peacefully eating a sandwich on what appears to be her lunch break. Presently, she scratches her left earlobe. You now approach that person and ask,

2.4. Excuse me, but about that earlobe scratching that you did just a moment ago: was that something you did of your own free will?

I suspect that she will feel you're behaving strangely and perhaps that your question is an absurd one. This is some evidence that the traditional "free will problem" can only be formulated by abusing language in some way.

Ordinary Language philosophers in their heyday used analogous strategies in an effort to dissolve traditional problems about truth, the mind–body problem, theological discourse, knowledge, and many other topics. By the mid-1950s it was looking like there would be rather little left of traditional philosophy. However, within a decade the Ordinary Language movement was facing severe obstacles. The first of these stems from the fact, as we pointed out in Section 2.1 in discussing semantic compositionality, that meanings compose to produce more complex meanings in a systematic way. (For the moment we may remain agnostic as between the strong and weak versions of that compositionality thesis.) Recall that Ayer had claimed that in calling an action wrong I am not making a statement about it, but am merely evincing my disapproval of it. On closer scrutiny this thesis turns out to be ambiguous, depending on how we construe the notion of calling. To explain this ambiguity, I will consider the phenomenon of saying instead of that of calling. (This choice is for continuity with other topics of the book only.) Then consider the sentence:

Emotivist Claim: To say that an action is wrong is to evince one's disapproval of that action (or type of action).

Saying comes in two forms, one thick and the other thin. In the thin form, 'saying' means something like 'uttering meaningful words.' We exemplify this thin notion when we rehearse lines from a play or practice our elocution. We can do either of these things without speaker-meaning the words we utter. Let us use subscripts to refer to this thin notion: 'say$_{thin}$.' We also make use of a thicker notion of saying according to which speakers do speaker-mean the words they utter: "You said I should stop, so I did." Here the speaker is presuming that the person she is addressing not only uttered words but also speaker-meant them. Call this 'say$_{thick}$.'[7] Accordingly, the Emotivist Claim is ambiguous between two distinct claims:

> *Emotivist Claim* (thin): To say$_{thin}$ that an action is wrong is to evince one's disapproval of that action (or type of action).
>
> *Emotivist Claim* (thick): To say$_{thick}$ that an action is wrong is to evince one's disapproval of that action (or type of action).

The thick version of the Emotivist Claim is reasonably plausible, and in more sophisticated guises it has contemporary defenders.[8] However, the thin version of that claim yields controversial results. The reason is that we may easily construct examples in which someone says$_{thin}$ a sentence containing an "ethical symbol" without approving or disapproving of any course of action. For instance, one might say$_{thin}$ any of the following without evincing approval or disapproval of any course of action concerning euthanasia, addiction, or lying:

2.5. If suicide is wrong, then so is euthanasia.
2.6. I wonder if it's right to provide heroin addicts with clean needles.
2.7. Consider the following idea: sometimes it's right to lie.

Here is a dilemma for the emotivist: if she advocates the thin version of her doctrine, then her view would seem simply to be false (as examples 2.5–2.7 show). On the other hand, if she advocates the thick version of that view, then she will not be able to tell us what work ethical words are doing in contexts like 2.5–2.7. Further, it is natural to suspect that such an account will be obliged to ascribe a meaning to these words that is not exhausted by their role in expressing emotion. After all, words that are not ambiguous keep the same meaning whether they occur in a clause that is said$_{thick}$ or one that is said$_{thin}$.[9]

---

7. For the remainder of this book, I will generally continue to use these subscripts to indicate which notion of saying is at issue. In those cases in which the subscript is absent, that is because the distinction is not pertinent to the point being made.

8. van Roojen (2015) discusses modern descendants of the emotivist theory.

9. This objection to the emotivist theory is sometimes referred to as the Frege/Geach problem, in homage to the fact that it was implicit in insights had by Frege and was then explicated vigorously by P. Geach. (See van Roojen [2015] for references.) We will see another objection to the Ordinary Language movement in the work of P. Grice discussed in Chapter 4.

Donald Davidson crystallized many of the problems facing the Ordinary Language movement by arguing that its proponents had failed to appreciate the fact that once a bit of language acquires a stable meaning, that meaning is comparatively autonomous from its use in any particular act such as approving, asking, or denying. He termed this phenomenon the

> *Autonomy of Linguistic Meaning*: Once a feature of language has been given conventional expression, it can be used to serve many extra-linguistic ends; symbolic representation necessarily breaks any close tie with extra-linguistic purpose. (Davidson 1979, p. 113)

The Autonomy Thesis should not be interpreted so strictly as to imply that linguistic meaning can never change. Given what we learned about convention in Chapter 1, we should predict that if enough speakers begin to use a word w in a new way, and that pattern of usage matures into a convention, then w comes to have a new meaning. Nonetheless, the Autonomy Thesis tells us that at any given time, linguistic meaning floats comparatively free of the purposes of language users.

At the end of Section 2.3 we suggested that concepts might be better suited to help characterize linguistic meaning than are ideas. The Logical Empiricist improved upon the ideational theory by harnessing meaning to scientific method: prediction, observation, and experimentation are key in this approach to determining whether or not a bit of language is cognitively significant. However, we also found difficulties facing the Logical Empiricist: the self-application problem, the difficulty of de-lineating analytic from synthetic sentences, and the incompleteness of arithmetic together cast grave doubt on the theory. Its failure does not necessarily undermine the value of concepts, however, and in the next chapter we will see that an elucidation of concepts in terms of application (rather than verification) conditions is one promising route forward.

2.6. Study Questions and Suggestions for Further Reading

Study Questions

1. We suggested a way in which the Logical Empiricist could explain how interrogative sentences could be cognitively meaningful. Please consider whether the Logical Empiricist could also show how imperative sentences such as 'Shut the door' or 'Be on time' may

be meaningful. (Perhaps such sentences could be said to possess "practical meaning.")

2. Recall the self-application objection to the Logical Empiricists' doctrine LE1. Might the Logical Empiricist defend herself against it by showing that LE1 has a kind of meaning that is not cognitive? If so, what kind of meaning might that be?

3. In Section 2.4, we considered examples of sentences that seem to be meaningful but on closer inspection turn out not to be. Might there be sentences that seem not to be meaningful but on closer inspection turn out to be? (*Hint*: up in the Dakotas, people like to say that Buffalo buffalo buffalo buffalo.)

4. Could the Logical Empiricist generalize her strategy for understanding ethical discourse in terms of emotive meaning, to an analogous account of aesthetic and/or theological discourse? Please explain your answer.

5. Proponents of the meaning-as-use doctrine tend to draw an analogy between using language and playing a game. In what significant ways are these two activities analogous? Do they differ in significant ways as well? Please explain your answer.

Further Reading (with recommended [*] for instructors)

Book III of Locke's *Essay Concerning Human Understanding** is a locus classicus of an ideational theory of meaning. Davis (2003) offers a modern defense of an ideational theory that stands up against many of the objections that undermined earlier versions. Ayer's "Critique of Ethics and Theology" (chapter six of his *Language, Truth, and Logic*) is a virtuoso attempt to show how important areas of noncognitive discourse still possess some sort of meaning. Richardson and Uebel (2007) contains a wide range of useful essays on aspects of logical empiricism. Rey (2017) provides an illuminating discussion of the analytic/synthetic distinction and Quine's criticism of it. Phillips et al. (2011) discuss illusions of meaningfulness in detail. Van Roojen (2015) offers an excellent discussion of the emotivist view of ethical discourse, while Camp (2018) does so with a focus on connections to the philosophy of language.

Green (1997) elucidates Davidson's thesis of the Autonomy of Linguistic Meaning and defends a qualified version of it. Soames (2003) covers many of the topics of this chapter in greater detail.

References

Ayer, A. J. 1936. *Language, Truth and Logic.* New York: Dover.

Berlin, I. 1939. "Verification." *Proceedings of the Aristotelian Society* 39: 225–248.

Bradley, F. H. (1914) 1994. "What Is the Real Julius Caesar?" In *Essays on Truth and Reality*; reprinted in *F. H. Bradley: Writings on Logic and Metaphysics*, edited by J. Allard and G. Stock. Oxford: Oxford University Press, pp. 323–329.

Camp, E. 2018. "Metaethical Expressivism," Edited by T. McPherson and D. Plunkett, *Routledge Handbook of Metaethics* (New York: Routledge), pp. 87–101.

Carnap, R. (1935) 1966. *Philosophy and Logical Syntax.* London: Theommes Press.

Davidson, D. 1979. "Moods and Performances." Reprinted in his *Inquiries into Truth and Interpretation,* 109–121. Oxford: Oxford University Press.

Davis, W. 2003. *Meaning, Expression and Thought.* Cambridge: Cambridge University Press.

Green, M. 1997. "On the Autonomy of Linguistic Meaning." *Mind* 106: 217–244.

Hume, D. (1777) 1975. *An Enquiry Concerning Human Understanding.* Edited by P. H. Nidditch. Oxford: Oxford University Press.

Locke, J. 1690. *An Essay Concerning Human Understanding.* Edited by P. H. Nidditch. Oxford University Press.

Mill, J. S. 1882. *A System of Logic.* London: Harper & Brothers.

Phillips, C., Wagers, M., and Lau, E. 2011. "Grammatical Illusions and Selective Fallibility in Real-Time Language Comprehension." Edited by J. Runner. *Syntax and Semantics* 37: 147–180.

Quine, W. V. O. 1951. "Two Dogmas of Empiricism." *Philosophical Review* 60: 20–43.

Rey, G. 2017. "The Analytic/Synthetic Distinction." In *The Stanford Encyclopedia of Philosophy*, edited by Edward Zalta. https://plato.stanford.edu/entries/analytic-synthetic/

Richardson, A., and Uebel, T. 2007. *Cambridge Companion to Logical Empiricism.* Cambridge: Cambridge University Press.

Smith, P. 2007. *An Introduction to Gödel's Theorems.* Cambridge: Cambridge University Press.

Soames, S. 2003. *Philosophical Analysis in the Twentieth Century, Vols. I–II.* Princeton, NJ: Princeton University Press.

van Roojen, M. 2015. *Meta-Ethics: A Contemporary Introduction.* New York: Routledge.

CHAPTER 3
....

Linguistic Meaning
and Truth Conditions

Chapter Overview

We begin with a problem that the philosopher W. V. O. Quine (1908–2000) called *Plato's Beard*. After formulating the problem, I will then explain how Bertrand Russell (1872–1970) responded to it with the aid of formal techniques that had been recently developed by logicians such as Gottlob Frege (1848–1925). Explaining Russell's new solution will bring us to the topic of descriptions—both definite and indefinite. Finally, we will put together what we have learned into a formulation of the truth-conditional approach to meaning, which became an influential framework in the twentieth century and continues to play a major role in theorizing about linguistic meaning to this day. As we will see in Chapter 4, pragmatics got its start in opposition to this formalist tradition.

3.1. Speaking of Nothing

We approach a more defensible characterization of meaning than those considered in the last chapter by considering a problem and seeing what tools we need to help solve it. As mentioned in Chapter 1, we seem to be able to talk about things that do not exist. In telling you about the Greek deity Poseidon, for instance, I might mention that in an attempt to win the favor of the goddess Demeter, he created horses. Let's leave aside the

50

question of whether what I say about Poseidon, Demeter, and horses is true: while remaining agnostic on that issue, you can understand my remark in full awareness that neither Poseidon nor Demeter exists now or ever did exist in the past. But according to an ancient way of thinking about language, speakers use nouns (including proper nouns) to refer to things and use verbs to make comments about the things thus referred to. But if Poseidon is merely mythological, we might well wonder how we can refer to him in order to comment, for instance, that he created horses. After all, you probably doubt that a thorough investigation of the world's oceans would turn up any trident-wielding deities.

Similarly, the country of Iceland is no monarchy; instead, it is a parliamentary republic. Now imagine someone who says,

3.1. The current Queen of Iceland is rich.

Our speaker has apparently failed to say something true. But she has still said something meaningful: we know what it would be for the speaker's utterance to be correct. (We might imagine Iceland having a different political history and the current monarchy playing a largely symbolic role such as is found in Spain.) In this way, (3.1) is different from

3.2. Elocution trees angioplasty.

Although made up of meaningful words put together grammatically (assuming that 'trees' is used as a transitive verb), (3.2) leaves us puzzled as to what situations would show it to be true or false. But (3.1), which by contrast is meaningful, would seem to be so only if all the expressions within that sentence are meaningful as well. And yet, if one of those constituent expressions, 'The current Queen of Iceland' is meaningful, how can it be except by referring to something?

The Austrian philosopher Alexius Meinong (1853–1920) made the problem of referring to nonexistent things vivid in the latter part of the nineteenth century. Here is a crystallization of his argument that we might call

Plato's Beard

1. (3.1) is meaningful.
2. (3.1) can only be meaningful if any noun phrases it contains are themselves meaningful.
3. (3.1) contains the following noun phrase: 'the current Queen of Iceland.'

4. The noun phrase 'the current Queen of Iceland' is meaningful. (From 1, 2, and 3)
5. The only way in which this noun phrase could be meaningful is by referring to something.

Ergo,

6. There must in some sense be a current Queen of Iceland.[1]

This argument has a surprising conclusion that goes against our commonsense view that Iceland has no current queen. Meinong tried to mitigate the surprise of the conclusion by suggesting a distinction between those objects that do, and those that do not, have being. According to this distinction, anything that can be spoken or thought of is an object: Poseidon, the current Queen of Iceland, the largest integer, the Crab Nebula, and my cousin's deceased pet frog, Maurice, are all objects. But only some of these have a location in space and time, and these are the ones that have being. So Meinong would say that there is more in the world of objects than is found in the spatiotemporal world. We may illustrate Meinong's thought with the Venn diagram in Figure 3.1, according to which, all beings are objects, but there are objects that are not beings. These objects that are not beings have no causal powers. However, such objects still have *some* kind of reality, and Plato's Beard is supposed to show that unless they did so, it would be impossible to speak meaningfully about them.

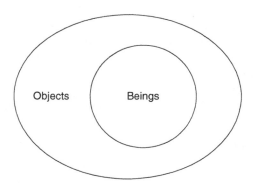

FIGURE **3.1 Meinong's distinction between objects and beings**

---

1. This argument is inspired by one of a similar form given in Strawson (1950).

In his earliest thought about Plato's Beard and the ontological picture it suggested, Russell (1903) found them both compelling. However, with time Russell became dissatisfied with them on account of their seeming to violate a methodological dictum known as Ockham's Razor: do not multiply entities beyond necessity.[2] Russell formulates the idea with reference to our current problem:

> many logicians have been driven to the conclusion that there are unreal objects. It is argued, e.g., by Meinong, that we can speak about "the golden mountain," "the round square," and so on; we can make true propositions of which these are the subjects; hence they must have some kind of logical being, since otherwise the propositions in which they occur would be meaningless. In such theories, it seems to me, there is a failure of that feeling for reality which ought to be preserved even in the most abstract studies. (1919, p. 169)

In the interests of parsimony, Russell wondered if there might be a way of accounting for our ability to use meaningful sentences that seem to refer to Poseidon, Demeter, and Icelandic monarchs without our having to posit objects that lack being.

3.2. Quantifiers and Other Logical Constants

To appreciate the novelty and power of Russell's approach, it is useful first to consider the concept of quantification. Think of quantifiers as devices whose job is to help answer questions of the form 'How many?,' 'How much?,' 'How fast?,' and so on. Such expressions as 'all dogs,' 'few doctors,' and 'most Ukranians,' are among the quantifiers in English. Sentences containing such quantifiers exhibit a distinctive logical structure that does not easily conform to the traditional conception of language tracing back to Aristotle (384–322 BCE). For him, the basic function of a sentence is to pick out an object and to say something about it. He puts this point succinctly when in *On Interpretation* he says,

> An affirmation is a positive assertion of something about something. (2017, p. 82)

In speaking of an "assertion of something about something," Aristotle is alluding to the idea that in making an affirmation, a speaker picks

---

2. For further discussion, see Keele (2010).

out an object (a horse, a trireme, or even a city) and then goes on to say something about it (that it is speedy, or dangerous, or crowded).

Aristotle's model may be a good one for many sentences. However, it is not clear how it will apply to a sentence such as

3.3. All dogs are mammals.

Traditional grammar might construe this as a sentence whose noun phrase (hereafter 'NP') is 'All dogs' and whose verb phrase (hereafter 'VP') is 'are mammals.' In that spirit, the Aristotelian approach would have us see the NP ('all dogs') in this sentence as functioning to pick something out before the VP ('are mammals') says something about it. But what kind of entity might 'all dogs' refer to?[3] A natural answer to this question is: all dogs, or more specifically, the set of all dogs. However, if that were correct, then should not the earlier sentence be singular rather than plural? After all, on this hypothesis, the NP refers to a single individual, albeit one that has many members, namely the set of all dogs. Further, this set is not a mammal; its members are. Brief reflection will show that things get even stranger when we try to apply the Aristotelian model to a sentence such as 'No dogs bark.'

New logical tools developed in the latter part of the nineteenth century provide a way out of this thicket. With the aid of such tools, the earlier sentence may be understood as saying,

3.4. For all x such that x is a dog, x is a mammal.

We may put this more succinctly by using some modern notation that is itself a refinement of those nineteenth-century tools. Let us read '$\forall x$' as an abbreviation for 'for all x' and '$\exists x$' as an abbreviation for 'for some x.' Where 'Φ' names a property, such as being a dog or being a mammal, we will also use '$\Phi(x)$' to abbreviate 'x has the property of being a Φ,' or more colloquially, 'x is Φ.' ('$\forall x$' and '$\exists x$' are known as the universal and existential quantifier, respectively, and 'Φ' is known as a one-place predicate.) Now we write,

3.5. [$\forall x$: Dog(x)](Mammal (x))

---

3. Aristotelian logic did possess the resources to express propositions of the form, *All A's are B's*. However, it was not until the nineteenth century and the work of Gottlob Frege that systems were developed with the expressive power to capture such propositions as *For all x, there is a y such that that for all z*, etc. See Smith (2017) for a discussion of Aristotle's logical systems.

or more colloquially, anything that is a dog is also a mammal. It is therefore a purely general sentence, saying of any object that is a dog, that it is also a mammal. Because you know the conditions under which this sentence is true, you would seem to understand it. But you may do *that* while remaining neutral on the question whether there are any dogs. (That, after all, is a question for biology, not philosophy, to settle.) Other quantifier phrases do permit us to make existential commitments. For instance, intuitively you can see that 'Some dogs are mammals' commits its user to the conclusion that there are some dogs. Analogous remarks may be made for 'most dogs' and 'few dogs':

Some dogs are mammals	$[\exists x: Dog(x)](Mammal\ (x))$
Most dogs are mammals	$[Most\ x: Dog(x)](Mammal\ (x))$
Few dogs are mammals	$[Few\ x: Dog(x)](Mammal\ (x))$

Certain other quantificational terms may be understood as combinations of these and other logical concepts. For instance, rather than posit a new quantifier, 'No x,' we may understand sentences containing negation as combinations of 'all,' 'not' (symbolized here as '¬'), and other nonlogical material on the following pattern:

No dogs are mammals	$[\forall x: Dog(x)](\neg(Mammal\ (x)))$

The present apparatus also helps us shed light on structural ambiguity. One such ambiguity is generated by the interaction of quantifiers and negation. The sentence 'All cats don't chase mice' could be used to say either that not all cats chase mice (which leaves open the possibility that some do), or that all cats fail to chase mice (which rules out that possibility). It is, however, difficult to keep track of this distinction with only the expressive devices of natural language, and our new tools prove their value in laying it bare. They do so by rendering the two sentences as:

$\neg([\forall x: Cat(x)]((Mice$- chasing $(x)))$	$[\forall x: Cat(x)](\neg(Mice$- chasing $(x)))$

This rendering in turn makes clear that the sentence on the right is logically stronger than (that is, entails but is not entailed by) the sentence on the left. That the logical explication of quantifiers can help us to bring to the surface an ambiguity that we find in natural language is evidence in favor of that explication. This in turn is reason to think that sentences such as these do not contain any referring expressions, nor should we be misled by an argument along Meinong's lines into

TABLE **3.1 Some Quantificational Sentences, Their Logical Formulations, and Their Truth Conditions**

Sentence	Logical notation	Truth conditions
Some dogs are mammals.	[∃x: Dog(x)](Mammal (x))	There is at least one dog that is also a mammal.
All dogs are mammals.	[∀x: Dog(x)](Mammal (x))	Anything that is a dog is also a mammal.
Most dogs are mammals.	[Most x: Dog(x)](Mammal (x))	Over half of dogs are mammals.
Few dogs are mammals.	[Few x: Dog(x)](Mammal (x))	Under half of dogs are mammals.
No dogs are mammals.	[∀x: Dog(x)](¬(Mammal (x)))	Nothing is both a dog and a mammal.
All cats don't chase mice.	¬([∀x: Cat(x)](Mice-chasing (x))) or [∀x: Cat(x)](¬(Mice-chasing)(x))	Some cats are non-mice-chasing; or All cats are non-mice-chasing.

concluding that the realm of Objects contains such things as "nondogs." Table 3.1 shows how our understanding of quantifiers provides an alternative to the traditional Aristotelian approach to all sentences in terms of nouns and verbs.

Here are some tricky questions that arise as we contemplate the accuracy of these elucidations. First of all, our truth conditions for a sentence such as 'Some dogs are strong swimmers' has the consequence that this sentence would be true even if all dogs were strong swimmers. However, when a speaker remarks, "Some dogs are strong swimmers," she is often understood as suggesting that not all dogs are strong swimmers. Should we therefore interpret 'Some a's are b's' as having truth conditions captured by the condition that some but not all a's are b's? If not, what alternatives might be available for addressing this fact about conversational practice?

Second, our truth conditions for sentences like 'Everyone had fun!' as said in response to the question 'How did your party turn out?' would seem to be,

([∀x: Person(x)]((Had fun at the party (x))).

But, of course, in answering as you do, you are not claiming that every person on the planet came to your party and had fun. Might there be some way of reassigning truth conditions to get them to match up more closely to what you likely meant in this case? Alternatively, might we be justified in suspecting that you were not speaking literally in answer to your friend's question about the party? Perhaps you were being hyperbolic in a way that we often are when speaking loosely, such as when we describe ourselves as "starving" when we're merely hungry, and "freezing" when we are merely chilly. We will return to this question in Chapter 6.

Not only does the truth-conditional approach to meaning characterization show us how to resist unwanted ontological conclusions, it also suggests a strategy for other areas of language. Suppose that we find compelling the suggestion that the sentences in the left column of Table 3.1 have their meaning fully characterized by the columns to their right. We might then try to generalize that strategy. In particular, other so-called logical constants are terms such as 'or,' 'and,' 'if ... then ...,' 'not,' and '... if and only if ....' Consider the word 'and.' I suspect you will find it difficult to specify an object that would serve as a reasonable candidate to count as its meaning. But by now you should not feel bothered by this failure. Instead, you are in a position to see that this word's meaning may be fully characterized by specifying the truth conditions of the sentences in which it occurs, and those truth conditions may be specified quite simply as:

The sentence 'A and B' is true if and only if 'A' is true and 'B' is true.[4]

We may follow a similar strategy for 'or' as follows:

The sentence 'A or B' is true if and only if either 'A' is true or 'B' is true.

And for 'not':

The sentence 'not-A' is true if and only if 'A' is not true.

Upon first inspection, these characterizations may seem circular. However, we should note that they are not intended to provide an understanding of the sentence on the left side of the 'if and only if' to someone who does not know English. If you have sufficient mastery of this language, you already know what 'and,' 'or' 'not,' and other logical constants mean. These biconditional sentences (or 'biconditionals' for short) are

---

4. The astute reader might object to this characterization by pointing out that someone who says, "Ahmad took the medicine and got better" would seem to be saying something different from "Ahmad got better and took the medicine." We will address this issue in Chapter 6. For now, however, you might reflect on the following question: is the difference between the two utterances due to a difference in what is said or to a difference in *how* that it is said?

TABLE 3.2 Sentences Containing Logical Constants, Their Logical Notations, and Their Truth Conditions

Sentence	Logical notation	Truth conditions
A or B	A v B	Either A is true or B is true
A and B	A & B	Both A and B are true
If A, then B	A -> B	Either A is false or B is true
Not A	¬A	A is not true
A if and only if B	A ≡ B	Both A and B are true, or both A and B are false

instead intended to bring to the surface what you already know about the terms being elucidated. Table 3.2 organizes this knowledge.

Our question is now: armed with the logical tools we have just introduced, does the truth-conditional approach apply, and apply adequately, to other areas of language? Two extensively discussed topics are descriptions and proper names, to which we turn in the remainder of this chapter, and then the next chapter, respectively.

BOX 3.1   TRUTH VALUES AND TRUTH CONDITIONS

Truth values and truth conditions are related but distinct concepts with different explanatory roles to play in the characterization of linguistic meaning. In this book we will assume that every meaningful indicative sentence always has exactly one of the following truth values: true or false (sometimes abbreviated T and F, respectively). (Some more advanced treatments of linguistic meaning will relax this assumption.) By contrast, a sentence's truth conditions consist in the pattern of truth values from one possible situation to another. It is common practice in the study of linguistic meaning to look to truth conditions rather than truth value as a superior tool for analyzing linguistic meaning. The following two sentences both have the truth value of True: '2 + 7 = 9' and 'Aristotle was a philosopher.' However, they have different truth conditions. The reason is that while '2 + 7 = 9' is true in all possible situations, 'Aristotle was a philosopher' is not: As we will see in Chapter 4, it seems that the person picked out by the name 'Aristotle' might not have chosen the life of the mind, but become a sculptor or farmer instead. In such a situation, 'Aristotle was a philosopher' would be false. Thus, in spite of their identical truth values, '2 + 7 = 9' and 'Aristotle was a philosopher' have different truth conditions. That fits nicely with the strong intuition that these two sentences differ in meaning.

3.3. Descriptions

Suppose that I utter the following sentence after inspecting damage that has been done to our treehouse:

3.6. A woodpecker made holes in our treehouse.

Under what conditions would this sentence be true? Presumably, they are precisely those conditions in which at least one woodpecker made those holes. If all the holes were made by a gun or by termites, then what I have said is false. If two woodpeckers collaborated in the mischief, what I say would still be true, though perhaps misleading. Furthermore, while 3.6 is a meaningful sentence, it does not seem to be in the business of enabling speakers to refer to any particular bird: it does not pick out a particular woodpecker and say something about it. Rather, 3.6 is conventionally used to make a statement that is quite general, but no less precise for that. Accordingly, while it may be that on some grammatical characterizations 'a woodpecker' is an NP, its being meaningful does not depend on its referring to anything, whether to an object having being or not. For we may construe 3.6 as

3.7. There is at least one woodpecker that made holes in our treehouse.

Or even more perspicuously as

3.8. There is an x such that x is a woodpecker and x made holes in our treehouse.

Which in turn is expressed with the aid of our quantificational notation as

3.9. [∃x: Woodpecker(x)](Made-holes-in-our-treehouse (x)).

In moving from 3.6 to 3.9, we lay bare the deeper underlying structure of the former. Consequently, because (3.9) does not contain any NPs, this is reason to conclude that 3.6 only appears to contain them. That in turn would allow us to see that the argument we have called Plato's Beard would not apply to sentences such as 3.6. For indefinite descriptions, at least, no argument in the style of Plato's Beard is going to force us to conclude anything about the ontological status of woodpeckers. Of course, if 3.6 is true, that can only be if there is at least one woodpecker that did the mischief. However, the sheer fact that 3.6 is meaningful is not going to force any ontological conclusions upon us. The same point would apply, of course, to a sentence such as 'A goblin killed my cat.' We can acknowledge that the sentence is meaningful without being forced to conclude that there are any objects picked out by the phrase 'a goblin.'

Descriptions are phrases of the form 'an x,' or 'the x,' where 'x' is replaced by a count noun such as 'dog' or 'marble'; they can be singular (as in the previous examples) or plural ('x's,' 'the x's'), can take the form of genitives ('x's y,' as in 'Susan's broken vase,' which is a brief way of referring to a broken vase belonging to Susan), and can comprise mass nouns as well, as in 'The snow falling outside'; some proper names also wear descriptive clothing, as in 'The Danube,' or such as we find in the Californian way of referring to freeways: 'The 405.' Further the superficial grammatical form of a description-containing sentence does not always correspond directly to a particular meaning. For instance, not all expressions of the form 'an x' are accurately modeled with existential quantification. The sentence 'A blue whale calf drinks 100 gallons of milk per day' is not standardly used to say there is at least one such calf that drinks so much. Rather, this sentence is standardly used to make a general claim which may be more perspicuously stated as 'Typical blue whale calves drink ...' But note again that Meinong's style of reasoning will not gain much traction in such cases. To see why, consider an old dictum from the American South:

3.10. A haint cain't haint a haint.

'Haint' is Southern American English slang, meaning 'ghost' when used as a noun and meaning 'to haunt' when used as a transitive verb. Accordingly, 3.10 means that a ghost cannot haunt another ghost. We can acknowledge that the sentence is meaningful without thereby being committed to ghosts, even as objects lacking in being. For all 3.10 says is

3.11. For all x and y such that x and y are ghosts, x cannot haunt y.

We can see perfectly well what this sentence means without having to believe that the world in any sense contains ghosts.

You might by this point feel that while these observations are just fine as an account of indefinite descriptions like 'a woodpecker' and 'a ghost,' they do little to neutralize Meinong's argument as it applies to definite descriptions such as 'the current Queen of Iceland,' which we encountered in sentence 3.1. Might the meaningfulness of this phrase mandate positing a current Icelandic monarch? Russell thinks not, and to explain that answer he urges that a phrase of the form 'the soandso' is in important respects similar to 'a soandso,' The former merely adds a further condition to the existence condition that we have already encountered among indefinite descriptions. That is, 'The current Queen of Iceland is rich,' is analyzed as

> 3.12. There is at least one, and at most one, present, female Icelandic monarch, and whoever is a present, female Icelandic monarch is rich.

3.12 only adds a "uniqueness" condition to the "existence" condition that we already saw in the case of the indefinite description. But adding such a further condition will not turn a sentence that contained no NPs into one that does contain an NP. 3.12 is perfectly meaningful, and we know exactly the conditions under which it would be true. But it is also perfectly general, saying that a certain set of conditions are uniquely satisfied. If those conditions are uniquely satisfied, then the sentence is true; otherwise the sentence is not true.[5]

If Russell is right to "Russell away" appearances associated with sentences involving descriptions, then he will have done a good deal to use Ockham's Razor to shave Plato's Beard. Recall that this argument purports to show that the sheer meaningfulness of a sentence such as 3.1 implies the existence, or at least being, of a present Icelandic monarch. In undermining this argument, Russell does not think that he has thereby proven that such an entity does *not* exist. All he has done is relieve us of any need to posit such a thing on the basis of linguistic considerations alone. So, too, just as the fibers at the crime scene may not be enough to show that Smith is the culprit in the crime, he may still be the one who perpetrated the gruesome deed.

The Russellian analysis of indefinite and definite descriptions was influential in the first half of the twentieth century; indeed, Russell's contemporary Frank Ramsey went so far as to hail it as "a paradigm of philosophy." Russell's analysis is a good example of how clarification about the structure of language can help not so much to solve, but rather to *dissolve*, traditional philosophical problems. It even offers a suggestion as to why such problems have proven intractable: they were so hard to overcome because they rested on a confusion about our language!

---

5. For most purposes we may assume that not being true, and being false, are the same thing. However, some theorists have found reason to distinguish these notions, and when we come later on to speak of "truth value gaps," we will look into the issue more carefully. For now, however, we will not fuss over this distinction.

That confusion, it might be suggested, was brought on by our tendency to focus on expressions in isolation and asking what they mean. Instead, Russell teaches us, a wiser course is to observe how an expression contributes to the meaning of sentences in which it occurs, and to draw lessons about its meaning based on what we learn in doing so.[6]

Ambiguity: We have just introduced part of what came to be known as Russell's Theory of Descriptions. (I say only "part" because the full Theory also contains epistemological doctrines not pertinent to our considerations in this book, and which will be here left aside.) Russell's theory also relates in an illuminating way to the phenomenon of ambiguity. He will not claim that 'The current Queen of Iceland is rich' is ambiguous, either lexically or structurally. However, Russell points out that we do encounter ambiguity in the presence of negation. Consider for instance:

> 3.13. The current Queen of Iceland is not rich.

This could be read either as

> 3.14. There is at least one, and at most one, current Queen of Iceland, and whoever is a current Queen of Iceland is not rich,

or instead as

> 3.15. It is not the case that there is at least one, and at most one, current Queen of Iceland who is rich.

3.14 is true only if Iceland is currently a monarchy, while 3.15 does not have this condition on its truth. As a result, these two disambiguations do not mean the same thing. Rather than take this fact to be an objection to his theory, Russell may take it to be a virtue. The reason, he could urge, is that 3.13 is itself ambiguous, and so a theory that attempts to spell out its meaning ought to predict that it is. Russell's position does this nicely.

Generics: In a manner analogous to our blue whale calf example, not all uses of 'the' purport to say that there is at least and at most one

---

6. One sometimes hears in this regard a slogan known as the *context principle*. One formulation of that principle tells us that it is only in the context of a sentence that a word has any meaning. That formulation raises distracting controversies. Instead, we do better to adopt a heuristic version of that principle, which might run: A good way to understand a word's meaning is to observe how it contributes to the meanings of sentences in which it occurs.

thing with a certain property. For instance, a speaker who says, "The Komodo dragon hunts humans," might well mean to be speaking of all, or at least most Komodo dragons. Her utterance carries the same information as if she had said, "Komodo dragons hunt humans," which we may in turn try to explicate in either of the following ways:

3.16.   For all x such that x is a Komodo dragon, x hunts humans.

3.17.   For most x such that x is a Komodo dragon, x hunts humans.

Neither 3.16 nor 3.17 claims that there is at most one Komodo dragon that hunts humans. As with indefinite descriptions that may be used to make generalizations, this phenomenon need not trouble Russell, who may just note that here we have another of the many uses of "the soandso." We will see in Chapter 7 that generics are of independent interest.

Incomplete definite descriptions: Another issue merits closer attention. For consider how Russell's approach might apply to a piece of everyday discourse such as

3.18.   The book has a surprising ending.

I might say this about a book we both see as we stroll past a shop window. Apparently 3.18 will be true, on Russell's analysis, just in case there is at least one book, and at most one book, and that book has a surprising ending. But surely this is not what is typically being said by someone who utters 3.18! In the scenario in which we imagine my saying it, I would not find the following reply appropriate:

3.19.   Sorry, you're mistaken, because there is more than one book in the world.

It seems, however, that Russell's theory would predict that one could appropriately challenge my assertion by remarking that its "uniqueness" condition is not satisfied.[7]

Might the utterer of 3.18 be speaking elliptically? Consider a standard case of ellipsis:

3.20.   I enjoy horror stories; my children, mysteries.

---

7. Sentences such as 3.18 are known as "incomplete definite descriptions." This terminology seems to me misleading, since it suggests controversially that such descriptions are in some way in need of completion. However, students wishing to research this topic in further depth will need to use the established terminology, and so I shall continue to employ it here.

3.20 has had the verb 'enjoy' elided from it. Nevertheless, a speaker who uses this sentence literally and to make a statement would appear to be saying among other things that her children enjoy mysteries. More generally, an elided part of an utterance is still part of what a speaker says in that utterance. (This is true for both the thin and thick senses of 'say.') One symptom of a bit of information having been elided from a sentence is that another speaker can refer to it with a pronoun: "Do they?" in response to 3.20 is naturally heard as asking for confirmation that one's children like mysteries. Analogous remarks apply to "Yes, they do" or "They sure do," in response to that sentence.

Given this background, our question is whether incomplete definite descriptions contain elided material in a way similar to 3.20. Perhaps the speaker of 3.18 is really saying something like

3.21. The book that we can both see has a surprising ending.

(Assume that the speaker thinks both she and her addressee can see the book in question.) However, this posit of elided material is not borne out by our test: "Yes, we can" or "Can we?" cannot be heard as asking, in response to an utterance of 3.18, whether we can both see the book under discussion. Further, you can probably think of cases in which there is more than one book that is visible to the speaker and her addressee, but where the speaker has no problem getting her point across by saying 3.18.

Even if the further specification of the description is not part of what the speaker says, albeit elliptically, might it nevertheless be part of what she means, in the sense of speaker-meaning? We have already observed (Chapter 1) that speakers often mean more, or instead something quite different, from what they say. As the server in a restaurant spills gazpacho over my shirt, I remark, "Nice job," saying that he did a nice job but meaning that the job he did was not so nice. So, too, perhaps the aforementioned explication expresses what the speaker of 3.18 meant even if it is not what she said.

Some support for this way of seeing matters comes from the fact that another speaker might ask, "Which book do you mean?" and receive a reply such as "Oh, I meant the one on the middle shelf next to the ramen cookbook." This is not so different from what might be needed to clarify my use of a proper name that has more than one bearer: "Which Joe Smith are you speaking about?"

Another approach to incomplete definite descriptions holds that speakers normally presume, as a background parameter of their conversations, a *domain of discourse*, a subset of all the things that exist, that has the further feature of being shared, and acknowledged as shared, by speakers and their addressees. On this approach, the quantifiers that according to Russell's analysis are implicit in the logical structure of many of the sentences that we utter, only range over items in that domain. The hypothesis that speakers and their addressees normally assume an implicit domain of discourse would help to explain why, at the beginning of a foot race when someone calls out, "All runners at the starting line," we would not expect to hear the reply, "Wait, do you mean all runners in the world?" So, too, the hypothesis of an implicit domain of discourse would help account for the ease of interpreting a typical utterance of 3.18.

Presupposition failure: It might also be objected that Russell's account of descriptions makes incorrect predictions in a different way. For his analysis of 3.1 seems to predict that if that sentence is asserted in a world in which Iceland is no monarchy, then we would judge it to be false; after all, one of its truth conditions is not satisfied. However, as a matter of fact—the objection goes—in such a situation we would not judge it false so much as respond with something more dramatic like "Sorry, but you must be under some misapprehension; Iceland is not a monarchy." Another speaker might point out that the question of that sentence's truth does not so much as arise. P. Strawson (1950), who is credited with formulating this objection to Russell, has gone so far as to say that in a world in which Iceland is no monarchy, the sentence is neither true nor false!

Russell was not much concerned with how well his theory of descriptive sentences would square with the intuitions of everyday speakers; this becomes clear in his response to Strawson (Russell 1957). Nonetheless, students of language as used in everyday discourse were struck by Strawson's observation, which brought to the surface the notion of presupposition. In its earliest formulation, scholars understood this notion as a precondition that needs to be satisfied in order for a sentence to be either true or false. However, as we shall see in Chapter 5, more recent work on the topic of presupposition sees it as pertaining to conditions that must be satisfied in order for an utterance to be conversationally *appropriate*. Even before a fuller discussion of presupposition, it may be clear that an utterance can be true but conversationally inappropriate. So, too, an utterance might be false, but also so inappropriate that it fails to rise to the level of a "speech act" in the sense of that term to be developed in Chapter 4.

Referential and attributive: Another potential objection to Russell's approach contends that we sometimes use definite descriptions referentially, that is, to pick out a particular individual that may not even satisfy the conditions expressed by the description. I spot a woman several yards away eating what I believe to be a hamburger, and I say to my friends,

> 3.22. The woman eating a hamburger is into conspiracy theories.

Unbeknownst to me, the woman in question is eating a veggie burger. However, since she is the only one in the restaurant eating anything looking like a burger, my friends are nevertheless able to discern to whom I am referring. In fact, they will be able to do this even if they know that she is eating a veggie burger and not a hamburger.

On the basis of examples such as the previous, scholars such as Donnellan (1966) have concluded that definite descriptions have a "referential use." If this is merely the claim that in some cases, speakers are able to use definite descriptions to draw others' attention to an object even when that object does not satisfy the descriptive information they've used, the claim is, as we've seen, plausible. (One could just as plausibly point out that when I mistakenly refer to a fork as a 'spoon,' my interlocutors can sometimes discern what I had in mind and pass me the desired fork.) On the other hand, if we conclude from the hamburger/veggie burger case that definite descriptions are either lexically or structurally ambiguous, then it must at least be recognized that this is a dramatic conclusion from the evidence provided. None of us, I take it, would infer from the fork/spoon example that the word 'fork' is ambiguous. So, too, no reason emerges yet for positing an ambiguity in definite descriptions between "referential" and "attributive" uses. Speakers may do a great variety of things with words that go beyond their conventional meaning, but this behavior only becomes semantically significant if such uses become conventionalized.

3.4. Truth-Conditional Semantics and Linguistic Meaning

In appealing to truth conditions, we are not putting truth on a pedestal. In particular, we are not supposing that all truths are knowable or tethering meaning to verification conditions. Instead, we are thinking of truth in the most banal way possible. Does water boil at 212 degrees

Fahrenheit? Did Roman soldiers cross the River Danube in AD 212? How many oranges did Alycia carry in her backpack this morning? These are all everyday questions that admit of answers, some of which are true, while others are false. In some cases, such as that about the Roman soldiers, we may not be in a position to settle the question if all of the relevant documents and other evidence have been destroyed. Even then, however, it would seem that there is a fact of the matter whether Romans did that in AD 212.

While only sentences, and in particular indicative sentences, have truth conditions, other parts of speech may be understood in light of how they contribute to those truth conditions. Consider the descriptive phrase 'Radika's cat.' This, we might say, refers to a particular object, a mammal that spent the morning in Radika's kitchen, to be exact. Consider also some properties, characteristics that things may or may not have, such as purring, weighing one kilo, or being hungry. When whatever is referred to or expressed by 'Radika's cat' is combined with, say, the property of bring hungry, we get a proposition, which in English is expressed by the sentence 'Radika's cat is hungry.' That proposition is true or not depending on the condition of a particular cat. More generally, NPs and VPs have meanings that "fit" together in systematic ways to form sentences, and those sentences in the indicative mood are in turn true or false depending on how things are.

While truth conditions shed light on an important dimension of linguistic meaning, many have doubted that they can tell us all we need to know about it. Two sentences might have the same truth conditions and yet differ on some level pertinent to their meaning. 'A picked up the trash' and 'A picked the trash up' have the same truth conditions—there is no circumstance in which one is true but the other not. They would seem to differ stylistically only. However, other pairs of sentences are more puzzling.

3.23. John ate all the cookies.
3.24. It was John who ate all the cookies.

The second of these, known as an it-cleft sentence, would be appropriate to utter in a situation in which it has already been established that someone ate all the cookies and we are trying to figure out who it was. This is not so of the first, which might appropriately be used to introduce into our conversation the information that someone ate all the cookies. This difference, however, is not easily captured with a difference in truth conditions: in a situation in which John was indeed the cookie-eating culprit, but no one but myself knows that all the cookies have been eaten, my utterance of 3.24 might raise some eyebrows but would still seem to be true.

Here is another question for the truth-conditional approach to linguistic meaning. Linguists generally agree that the three major grammatical moods of the world's languages are the indicative, the imperative, and the interrogative. In Chapter 2 we considered whether the logical empiricist could count some sentences in the latter two moods (imperative and interrogative) as being linguistically meaningful even if they don't admit of empirical confirmation or disconfirmation. For the interrogatives, we suggested that rather than demanding empirical means of confirmation or disconfirmation, we require empirical means of *answerhood*. (We left as a study question how one might approach imperatives.) Now that we have found the empiricist criterion of linguistic meaning to be too restrictive, we have liberalized the test in terms of truth conditions. But little else changes. After all, we would seem to know what a question ("How many apples are in the bowl?" or "Who was the last person to use the copy machine?") means by virtue of knowing what would count as an answer to it. What would you try for imperatives?

3.5. Study Questions and Suggestions for Further Reading

Study Questions

1. Consider the sentence 'No dogs bark.' Can it be reasonably be analyzed as having an NP, VP structure? Please explain your answer.

2. We have analyzed 'No dogs are mammals' as [∀x: Dog(x)] (¬(Mammal (x)). How would you use the apparatus of quantifiers we have introduced to analyze 'Two dogs barked'?

3. We have noted that 'All cats don't chase mice' is ambiguous as between two readings: (i) ¬([∀x: Cat(x)]((Mice-chasing (x))), and (ii) [∀x: Cat(x)](¬(Mice-chasing (x))). We have also noted that (ii) entails (i) but not vice versa. Please establish these two claims. (Assume in your reasoning that there is at least one cat.)

4. We have noted that a typical utterance of 'Some dogs are strong swimmers' is typically taken to imply that some dogs are not strong swimmers. Should that further implication be built into the truth

conditions of 'Some dogs are strong swimmers'? Please explain your answer.

5. Please construct two scenarios in which a speaker makes an utterance that is true but conversationally inappropriate.

6. In Section 3.4 we considered two sentences (3.23 and 3.24) that have the same truth conditions but that seem to differ in their linguistic meaning. Please formulate another pair of sentences, not involving any it-cleft constructions, that similarly have identical truth conditions but that seem to differ in meaning.

7. Even if imperative sentences do not have truth conditions, perhaps we can use the method of truth conditions to provide them with something similar without making too dramatic a departure from that method. What would you suggest?

Further Reading (with recommended [*] items for instructors)

Altshuler, Parsons, and Schwarzschild (2019)* is an elegant and rigorous introduction to formal semantics requiring no prior background in the subject. Grossman (1974) is a careful treatment of Meinong's views. Russell (1919)* is a lucid exposition of his theory of descriptive phrases, and it is more accessible than his more famous 1905 article "On Denoting." Strawson (1950)* is a classic response to Russell. Neale (1990)* defends a powerful approach to descriptions largely in the spirit of Russell and against that of Strawson. Ostertag (1998) contains both classic and more recent articles on descriptions. Bezuidenhodt and Reimer (2004) also contains important work on descriptions, while Brogard (2014) is a helpful bibliographical essay on the topic. Ludlow (2018) surveys the topic at a more advanced level.

References

Altshuler, D., Parsons, T., and Schwarzschild, R. 2019. *A Course in Semantics.* Cambridge, MA: MIT Press.

Aristotle. 2017. "On Interpretation." In *Sourcebook in the History of the Philosophy of Language: Primary Texts from the Pro-Socratics to Mill,* edited by Cameron et al., 80–83. Berlin, Germany: Springer.

Bezuidenhodt, A., and Reimer, M. 2004. *Descriptions and Beyond.* Oxford, UK: Oxford University Press.

Brogard, B. 2014. "Descriptions." *Oxford Bibliographies Online.* (https://www.oxfordbibliographies.com/view/document/obo-9780195396577/obo-9780195396577-0032.xml?rskey=szidQF&result=73)

Donnellan, K. 1966. "Reference and Definite Descriptions." *Philosophical Review* 75: 281–304.

Grossman, R. 1974. *Meinong*. London: Routledge and Kegan Paul.

Keele, W. 2010. *Ockham Explained: from Razor to Rebellion* (Chicago: Open Court).

Ludlow, P. 2018. "Descriptions." In *Stanford Encyclopedia of Philosophy*, edited by Edward Zalta. https://plato.stanford.edu/entries/descriptions/

Neale, S. 1990. *Descriptions*. Cambridge, MA: MIT Press.

Ostertag, G. 1998. *Definite Descriptions: A Reader*. Cambridge, MA: MIT Press.

Russell, B. 1903. *The Principles of Mathematics*. New York: Norton.

Russell, B. 1919. "Descriptions." In his *Introduction to Mathematical Philosophy*. London: Allen and Unwin, pp. 167–180.

Russell, B. 1957. "Mr. Strawson on Referring." *Mind* 66: 385–389.

Smith, R. 2017. "Aristotle's Logic." *Stanford Encyclopedia of Philosophy*, edited by Edward Zalta.

Strawson, P. 1950. "On Referring." *Mind* 59: 320–344.

CHAPTER 4

Sense and Reference

Chapter Overview

In this chapter we continue our pursuit of characterization questions about linguistic meaning. A central proving ground for attempts to answer such questions is the semantics of proper names such as 'George Smith,' 'The Battle of Midway,' or '*An Affair to Remember.*' One reason for scholarly interest in proper names is that such expressions have seemed to be paradigmatic means by which our thoughts reach out to reality. Herein we will discuss two main theories of the semantics of names, known as Direct Reference and Fregean theories, associated with John Stuart Mill and Gottlob Frege, respectively. In the course of our discussion, we will develop and refine our account of linguistic meaning in terms of truth conditions.

4.1. Millian Heirs: The Theory of Direct Reference

Common sense has it that the central use of names is to refer to things, be they persons, cities, nations, or fictional characters. The great majority of entities in the universe lack names, while some have many. We are sometimes amused by the number of people in our acquaintance who share a name, as in Mike Doughty's song about going to school with 27 Jennifers.[1]

---

1. "I went to school with 27 Jennifers; 16 Jenns, 10 Jennies, and then there was her." From "27 Jennifers," © Mike Doughty.

Further, in spite of the conventional nature of the relation of a name to its bearer, there is a long tradition of thinking of names as somehow capturing a thing's essence.

Given the many pressures governing our uses of names, is there a way to characterize their meaning that is both accurate and general? A bracingly simple approach was forwarded by John Stuart Mill in his influential textbook, *A System of Logic* (1843). There Mill argues that a proper name's meaning is given entirely by its referent. That is, all one needs to know in order to understand the name 'Dartmouth' is that it refers to a particular English city. We also use the same series of letters to refer to an American college in New Hampshire, but many theorists will contend that there are two words here that happen to share identical orthography, rather than one ambiguous word. Mill remarks in addition that many proper names carry with them what are sometimes called connotations. For instance, 'Dartmouth' might carry with it the connotation that its bearer is located near the mouth of the River Dart. However, Mill contends that this connotation is no part of the meaning of the name. For suppose that the River Dart were to change its course due to an earthquake or the construction of a dam. We would not conclude that the city previously known as 'Dartmouth' no longer bears that name. Rather, we would still call Dartmouth by that name but possibly point out to first-time visitors that they will have to look elsewhere for the mouth of the river. Similarly, Mr. Armstrong may have frail arms, and the British indie band Royal Blood need have nothing royal about them.

Mill's bracingly austere doctrine has come to be known as

Direct Reference: The linguistic meaning of a proper name is given entirely by its referent.

Direct Reference has come in for heavy criticism. For instance, the theory implies that two proper names that refer to the same thing must have the same meaning. Given the principle of Strong Semantic Compositionality (defined in 2.1), Direct Reference also implies that two sentences that are just alike except one contains a name N1, and another contains N2, where N1 and N2 refer to the same entity, and where neither one is enclosed within quotation marks, will have the same meaning, and thus the same truth conditions. That is a hard pill to swallow. To see why, recall the Superman comic book series. In that story, you may remember, 'Superman' refers to a superhero, while 'Clark Kent' refers to a mild-mannered reporter employed by *The Daily Planet* newspaper. Unbeknownst to others, including Lois Lane, 'Superman' and 'Clark Kent' refer to one and the same person.[2] Because of her ignorance of the identity of Superman and Clark Kent, Lois thinks that the latter person is a reporter, but she would be astonished to be told that the former individual is. On the assumption that people are generally reliable authorities on what they believe, we may infer that 4.1 is true while 4.2 is not true.

4.1. Lois Lane thinks that Clark Kent is a reporter
4.2. Lois Lane thinks that Superman is a reporter.

A difference in truth values between 4.1 and 4.2, in turn, would imply that they have different truth conditions. Further, even if we are not yet convinced that sameness in truth conditions is sufficient for identity in linguistic meaning, it does seem to be a necessary condition for identity in linguistic meaning. It will follow, then, that 4.1 and 4.2 differ in their linguistic meaning. But given Strong Semantic Compositionality, and the assumption that 4.1 and 4.2 have the same grammatical structure, what could account for that difference in meaning except for a difference in the meanings of the proper names that they contain?

Consider also the phenomenon of empty names: these are proper names that are meaningful but which lack bearers. Apparently 'Zeus' and 'Superman' are empty names, and even outside of mythology, scientists have in the past posited entities and given them names only to find out that they are not real. (By contrast, 'Bandersnatch' from Lewis Carroll's poem "Jabberwocky" would seem not even to be meaningful: all we are told of the Bandersnatch in the poem is that it is frumious.) Direct Reference would seem to imply that empty names are meaningless. That would strongly suggest that a sentence such as

4.3. Superman wears a cape

---

2. Why not say that these two names refer to different aspects or stages of a single entity that is itself not accurately named by either name? One reason against this analysis is that it has difficulty making sense of how someone could come to realize that Superman and Clark Kent are one and the same person. The "two aspects" approach would be more plausible for cases in which multiple persons inhabit a single body, such as we find in Robert Louis Stevenson's story, "The Strange Case of Dr. Jekyll and Mr. Hyde." Jekyll and Hyde would seem to be distinct persons, and that would seem to show that their names do not refer to the same individual even though they inhabit the same body.

conveys no more information than does the sentence

    4.4. He wears a cape

uttered in a context in which no referent has been assigned to the pronoun. Yet we do sometimes want to make true, and thus meaningful
claims that contain empty names. An example is found in so-called
negative existentials. Suppose you come across a friend who is setting
out on a journey, and you ask her where she is headed. She replies that
she is off to find the city of Atlantis, having read great things about it in
an account by someone named Plato. With alarm, you reply,

    4.5. Hang on, Atlantis doesn't exist. It was a fictional island-state that
          Plato concocted for rhetorical purposes!

In asserting 4.5, you seem to be making a meaningful and, so far as we
know, true claim. But the Direct Reference theory seems to have trouble
making sense of this fact, given that to the best of our knowledge, there
is no entity to which 'Atlantis' refers.

    Further, it would appear that some claims that might be expressed
with names are known with no appeal to experience, while others are
not, and yet Direct Reference has trouble respecting the difference.
For instance, for someone who is competent with use of the name
'Hesperus,' the following sentence is one that she knows a priori,[3] or at
least can come to know it with minimal reflection:

    4.6. Hesperus is identical to Hesperus.

At the same time, even if she is competent with the co-referring name
'Phosphorus,' her knowledge of the truth of the following sentence is a
posteriori at best:

    4.7. Hesperus is identical to Phosphorus.

That, however, would only be possible if 4.6 and 4.7 do not mean the
same thing.

---

3. A proposition is a priori just in case it is known, or at least can be known, with no
appeal to experience. Once one knows the definition of a triangle, one knows, or can come
to know, that its internal angles add up to 360 degrees. For this reason, the proposition
'The internal angles of a triangle add up to 360 degrees' is a priori. A proposition is a posteriori just in case it is not a priori. As we saw in Chapter 2, a proposition's being known
a priori does not imply that it is known innately, nor does the reverse implication hold.

Gathering these objections together, then, we may say that Direct Reference has difficulties with (i) co-referential names occurring in attitude ascriptions (such as in 4.1 and 4.2), (ii) the apparent meaningfulness of sentences containing empty names (such as in 4.3), (iii) the apparent truth of some negative existential sentences (such as in 4.5), and (iv) capturing the distinctive a priori and a posteriori status of certain identity statements (such as in 4.6 and 4.7).

For much of the twentieth century, these objections to the Direct Reference theory seemed to many to be decisive. Indeed, the theory was sometimes lampooned under the title "The 'Fido'-Fido Theory of Meaning."[4] We will see in Section 4.4 that Direct Reference has in recent years been given a new lease on life, thanks to the ingenuity of some of its defenders. Before doing so, however, we will examine its main competitor.

4.2. Making Sense

In his famous essay "On Sense and Reference," Gottlob Frege (1848–1925) argues that a proper name's meaning has two components: its reference is one, but another is its *sense*, which he characterized as a mode of presentation of that referent. Given the history of the names 'Hesperus' and 'Phosphorus,' the former perhaps presents Venus as the first heavenly body seen in the evening, while the latter presents Venus as the last heavenly body seen before dawn. Competence with these names, for Frege, requires knowing not only what (if anything) they refer to but also the mode of presentation with which they are conventionally associated. So, too, returning to the Superman story, although 'Superman' and 'Clark Kent' co-refer, they present their referent in different modes or guises. The former presents him as a crime-fighting man of steel, while the latter presents him as a mild-mannered reporter. In contrast to what the Direct Reference theory would say of these names, the Sense/Reference theory would seem able to account for our view that these names do not mean the same thing. As we shall see in a moment, it would also seem able to account for the four phenomena adduced in the last section that seem to make trouble for Direct Reference.

The most influential method for characterizing sense is in terms of descriptions as developed in the last chapter, particularly in the framework of Russell's approach to descriptions. That is, Frege and Russell

---

4. See, for instance, Ryle (1949).

may join forces to claim that proper names of natural language are really disguised definite descriptions, with their truth conditions determined in the way that Russell proposed for such expressions. We know from Chapter 3 that a superficially simple sentence such as 'The dog chased a cat' hides a good deal of complexity when we try to unravel its underlying structure. Our suggestion now is that matters are not so different with sentences containing proper names, and this is precisely because those names behave as definite descriptions. Accordingly, a sentence such as

4.8.   Aristotle ate fish

has truth conditions that include descriptive information that ordinary speakers who are competent with the name 'Aristotle' may be expected to know, and that characterizes the man uniquely. Perhaps such truth conditions could be given as follows:

> There is at least one, and at most one individual who wrote *The Nichomachean Ethics*, studied under Plato, and served as tutor to Alexander the Great, and that individual ate fish.

(Observe that the names used in the explication would themselves need to be spelled out in descriptive terms as well.) More generally, we may contemplate a view such as the following:

> *Description Theory of Proper Names*: a proper name of ordinary language is semantically equivalent to a body of descriptive information that ordinary users competent with that name may be expected to know about the name's bearer; and those descriptions are uniquely satisfied by that bearer.

On this formulation, the Descriptive Theory of Proper Names (DTPN) does not tell you which definite description a given proper name is semantically equivalent to. In fact, finding an adequate description for a given proper name has turned out to be a challenge for proponents of DTPN. For the moment, however, notice that the DTPN has considerable initial appeal which we may highlight by reference to the four problems plaguing Direct Reference:

> (i) DTPN is consistent with the possibility of, and even begins to account for the behavior of co-referential names occurring in attitude ascriptions. For instance, it bids fair to account for how Lois Lane could believe that Clark Kent is a reporter without believing that Superman is. After all, she could coherently believe both

4.9. The mild-mannered person employed by the *Daily Planet* is a reporter.

4.10. The Lycra-clad superhero who protects our city from criminals is not a reporter.

It may be that the only way to discern that these two descriptions are satisfied by the same object is to gain a bit of a posteriori information to which Lois is not privy. For this reason, DTPN does not entail that 4.1 and 4.2 have the same truth conditions.

(ii) DTPN is also consistent with, and begins to make sense of, the apparent meaningfulness of sentences containing empty names such as in 4.3, for that sentence comes out as something like

4.11. The Lycra-clad superhero who protects our city from criminals wears a cape.[5]

Even if we do not believe that there is any individual answering to the description built into 4.11, we know its truth conditions, and thus, on the truth-conditional approach we have been articulating, we know its meaning.

(iii) Similarly, DTPN is consistent with and begins to make sense of the apparent truth of some negative existential sentences (such as in 4.5). For the sentence "Atlantis does not exist" comes out, according to DTPN, as something like

4.12. The city posited by Plato does not exist.

We know from Chapter 3 that sentences containing both negations and descriptions may be structurally ambiguous. Therefore, 4.12 may be glossed in either of two ways:

There is exactly one city such that ... and it does not exist
It is not the case that there is exactly one city such that ...

The first of these two sentences is meaningful but false. By contrast, the latter is not just meaningful but also, to the best of our knowledge, true, and it may therefore serve as an explication of what a speaker has in mind in uttering 4.5.

---

5. One might feel that in a certain sense, this sentence is not just meaningful, but it is also true, whereas, for instance, the sentence 'Superman tortures innocent children for fun' is false. However, we might make sense of this pattern of truth values by supposing that when we hear 4.11 as true, we are implicitly thinking of it as saying, 'In the superman story, the superhero who does ... wears a cape.'

(iv) Further, DTPN can capture the distinctive a priori and a posteriori status of certain identity statements (such as 4.6 and 4.7).
(This is the topic of a study question.)

There are yet more virtues of DTPN. For instance, DTPN is supported
by our everyday experience of learning new names. Imagine you over-
hear some people talking about someone named 'Tigranes,' and you
ask one of them who they're talking about. She replies, "Oh, he was the
second king of Armenia who reigned from 560 to about 535 BC." Perhaps another chimes in, "Yeah, he was part of the Orontid dynasty." That
descriptive information would seem to be more than enough to enable
you to use the name 'Tigranes' to refer to its bearer.

DTPN may also be harnessed to the tools of set theory to provide a
powerful and systematic approximation of meaning in natural language
in terms of truth conditions. Think of the conditions under which a
sentence is true as a set. One way to do this is in terms of Leibniz's
notion of a possible world, or possible state of affairs. We may understand possible worlds as the ways things either are or could have been.
Perhaps you are drinking some coffee while reading this book. Accordingly, the actual world is one in which you are drinking coffee. However,
you might have done something else: you can readily imagine that you
chose to have tea or carrot juice instead, or for that matter nothing at
all. Each of these three alternative possibilities represents another possible world. By contrast, there is no possible world in which you are
both drinking coffee and not drinking coffee at the same time: that's
an impossibility. Some metaphysicians will hold that there are also no
possible worlds at which you violate the laws of physics, for instance by
traveling faster than the speed of light. Luckily, this is a dispute that we
need not settle here.

In the possible-worlds framework, a set of truth conditions will
always be a subset (not necessarily proper) of the set of all possible
worlds. Two sentences have the same truth conditions just in case they
"carve out" the same set of possible worlds. 'Akira saw Stella,' for instance, carves out the same set of possible worlds as does 'Stella was
seen by Akira,' since there is evidently no possible world in which one
of these sentences is true and the other false. What is more, sentence
A entails sentence B just in case A's truth conditions are a subset of B's
truth conditions. A and B are compatible just in case their respective
truth conditions have a nonempty intersection; A and B are incompatible otherwise.

This approach can be extended to shed light on expressions that go to make up sentences. As we saw in the last chapter, we make larger sentences out of smaller ones with the help of connectives, which are words whose job it is to build larger sentences out of smaller ones in a recursive manner. Examples of connectives in English are 'and,' 'or,' 'not,' and 'if ... , then ...' Where A and B are sentences, we can make more complex sentences with the help of these connectives, to wit, 'A and B,' 'A or B,' 'Not A' (or 'It is not the case that A'), and 'If A, then B.' Further, the truth-conditional approach sheds light on the meanings of sentences so constructed. Where X is any proposition, let $||X||$ denote the conditions under which X is true. Then

$$||X\&Y|| = ||X|| \cap ||Y||$$
$$||XvY|| = ||X|| \cup ||Y||$$

According to the first formula, the truth conditions of X&Y are the intersection of the truth conditions of X with the truth conditions of Y; according to the second, the truth conditions of XvY are the union of the truth conditions of X and the truth conditions of Y. The truth-conditional approach tells us that these identities shed light on sentences having the form 'A and B,' 'A or B,' and so on. The reason is that the truth-conditional approach tells us that to determine the conditions under which 'A and B' is true, determine the truth conditions of each conjunct, A and B, and then take their intersection. Use the union operation for 'A or B,' and so on with appropriate modifications for the other connectives.

In addition to the sentential connectives, the truth-conditional approach also helps to shed light on how subsentential parts of speech contribute to the truth conditions of the sentences in which they occur. In philosophical parlance, a *predicate* is an expression that can be used to ascribe a feature to an object or set of objects. Predicates are sometimes one-place in the sense that they apply to sets of individuals: examples are 'x is red,' 'x hops faster than George,' 'x used to be my favorite kind of herring.' Other predicates are two-place, such as 'x is taller than y,' or 'x sees y.' The extension of these latter predicates will be a set of ordered pairs, particularly the set of pairs x and y such that x sees y. This pattern generalizes to three-place and thence to n-place predicates. (VP's are built out of predicates as well as possibly other grammatical material.) Generally, the *extension of predicate P, in situation w* is the set of things to which P applies in w. For one-place predicates, that will be a (possibly empty) set of individuals; for n-place predicates (n > 1) that will be a set of ordered n-tuples.

Noun phrases also have extensions. For convenience let us pretend for the moment that the meanings of the names 'George' and 'Samira' are given along the lines of Direct Reference, whence those meanings are exhausted by their referring to the entities that they do. So the extension of 'George' is, let us say, a certain frog, and the extension of 'Samira' is a certain rabbit. You may discern immediately that the extension of 'George' is not a member of the extension of 'hops faster than George,' since nothing can hop faster than itself. On the other hand, given plausible assumptions about rabbits, the extension of 'Samira' is a member of the extension of that predicate. That is, letting '$[[\alpha]]$' refer to the semantic value of 'α':

$[[George]] \notin [[hops\ faster\ than\ George]]$
$[[Samira]] \in [[hops\ faster\ than\ George]]$

As things are, there will be a certain number of entities that hop faster than George, among them, Samira. But we can imagine a situation, different from how things actually are, in which more things hop faster than George than actually do. Likewise, we can imagine a situation in which fewer things hop faster than George than actually do. What we have just done is imagine various possible worlds in which the extension of the predicate, 'x hops faster than George,' varies from one to the other. The same will be true for the other predicates we have considered. For every predicate you can formulate, so long as it is meaningful, it will have a (possibly empty) extension in the actual world, and it might have different extensions in different possible situations. Of course, some predicates will have the same extension across all possible worlds. One such is 'x is not identical with itself.' Since in every possible world, this predicate's extension is empty, it will have the same extension in all possible worlds, namely, the empty set, which we refer to with the term '$\varnothing$'.

To aid our thinking about the ways in which a part of speech might have one extension in possible world w1, another in possible world w2, and so on, we use the notion of an *intension*: while the extension of a part of speech at a world w is a set (either of individuals, or of ordered n-tuples of individuals), the *intension* of a part of speech is a function from worlds to extensions, that is, a function from worlds to sets.

The extension/intension distinction applies to noun phrases (NPs) as well as to predicates (or verb phrases). Consider the expression 'the winner of the 1903 Tour de France.' That description is satisfied by a particular individual, namely Maurice Garin. But it might have been satisfied by someone else. For suppose that Mr. Garin, the actual winner, had slipped on gravel during one of his descents and sustained an injury making him unable to continue the race. Then someone else, perhaps Lucien Pothier, might have won the contest instead. In that case, the NP 'The 1903 Tour de France winner' would have referred to another individual than the one to whom it does refer. Consequently, that NP has one extension in the actual world, but a different extension in other possible worlds. Here again, we will say that the extension of an NP, at a world, is a singleton, or set with only one member, and its intension will be a function from worlds to such sets. What is more, although 'Maurice Garin' and 'the winner of the 1903 Tour de France' have the same extension in the actual world, we have just seen that there are possible worlds in which they have different extensions. As a result, the intensions of these two NPs are different. This is one good way of articulating the intuitive idea that the two NPs differ in meaning in spite of referring to the same individual in the actual world. It is thus one way of developing Frege's sense/reference distinction.

An indication of the power of the extension/intension distinction is that it applies equally to both NPs and predicates. It even applies to whole sentences. Think of a sentence S as having an extension at a given possible world that is drawn from the set of possible truth values. For our purposes, that set will include only Truth and Falsity (abbreviated as T and F), though some more exotic forms of semantics will use other values. The intension of S will thus be a function from worlds to members of $\{T,F\}$.

We may sum up some of our main findings about extension and intension as in Table 4.1.

TABLE **4.1.** Extension and Intension for Some Major Grammatical Categories

Part of speech	Extension	Intension
NP	Singleton	Function from possible worlds to singletons
One-place predicate	Set of objects	Function possible worlds to sets
N-place predicate (where N > 1)	Set of n-tuples	Function from possible worlds to sets of n-tuples
Sentence	Member of the set {T,F}	Function from possible worlds to members of the set {T,F}

For verb phrases, noun phrases, and even sentences, then, we may distinguish extension and intension. Further, the notion of intension is often thought of as a *good first approximation of linguistic meaning*. That is, while two verb phrases might have the same extension in the actual world, the intension/extension distinction allows us to see that they might have different extensions in another possible world. To borrow an example from Putnam (1996), suppose that all and only creatures with hearts happen also to have kidneys. Then the VP 'is a creature with a heart' has the same extension as 'is a creature with a kidney.' But surely there is a possible world in which these two VPs have different extensions. Perhaps evolution might have gone differently in such a way that some creatures with hearts evolve a way of cleaning their blood with no aid of kidneys, and so these organs never manage to evolve in that lineage. Then the two VPs will have different intensions, even if they have the same extension in the actual world. But that is a good way of elucidating the intuitive idea that the two VPs 'is a creature with a heart' and 'is a creature with a kidney' do not mean the same thing. This contrasts with the relationship between 'x is a field with furze' and 'x is a field with gorse.' Assuming, as we noted in Chapter 1, that 'furze' and 'gorse' are two synonyms for a certain kind of ground covering, there is no possible situation in which these two terms would have different extensions. For it would seem that by definition, anything that is furze is also gorse, and vice versa. In that case, 'x is a field with furze' and 'x is a field with gorse' would also have identical intensions, unlike the case of 'is a creature with a heart' and 'is a creature with a kidney.'

In not too long we will see reason for doubting that the concept of intension makes all the distinctions we might like it to as we theorize about meaning. (It seems, that is, that there could be two sentences that we think of as having distinct meanings in spite of having identical intensions.) We will be able to address some of these concerns with further concepts that build atop that of intension. For now, however, the idea of truth conditions as intensions for the case of sentences is a useful first foray into linguistic meaning. It gives a clear and tractable interpretation of Frege's notion of sense. With the aid of set theory, it allows us to elucidate inferential relations among sentences, and it helps us to see how subsentential parts of speech compose to produce more complex semantic objects.

4.3. Objections to the Descriptive Theory of Names

The version of DTPN we have considered so far seems dramatically superior to Direct Reference. It meets desiderata (i)–(iv) set out earlier, while Direct Reference would seem able to meet none of them. Further, it suggests an account of how we learn names, as we saw in our example concerning Tigranes.

This virtue of the DTPN also suggests a qualification. For even if you associate the above name with the displayed description, other speakers may associate a different description with it. Think of contemporaneous subjects of King Tigranes. They might have known him as Tigranes, but many will have died before his reign was over, and many others may have been ignorant of which dynasty he came from. But Tigranes' prowess in archery was well known in his day, and so might have been part of the identifying information that such subjects knew him by. Perhaps this variation in descriptive information from one speaker to another is not an insurmountable problem, however. After all, even if two speakers attach different senses to a single name, this need not prevent them from being able to communicate so long as their two sets of descriptive information home in on the same object. Frege suggested just this in a well-known footnote to his famous article "On Sense and Reference," in which he writes,

> In the case of an actual proper name such as "Aristotle" opinions as to the sense may differ. It might, for instance, be taken to be the following: the pupil of Plato and teacher of Alexander the Great. Anybody who does this will attach another sense to the sentence "Aristotle was born in Stagira" than will a man who takes the sense of the name: the teacher of Alexander the Great who was born in Stagira. So long as the reference remains the same, such variations in sense may be tolerated, although they are to be avoided in a demonstrative science and ought not to occur in a perfect language. ([1892] 1970, p. 58)

Frege is assuming a distinction between an artificially constructed language such as we find in first-order predicate logic, and natural languages such as Swahili and Urdu. The former is what he would term a (logically) perfect language, and Frege famously holds that only such languages, which meet exacting standards, are appropriate for the conduct of rigorous science. In such languages, no name may be introduced unless it can be proven that it has a bearer. By contrast, Frege acknowledges that bearerless names occur in natural languages. Further, in such languages, when speakers use names that refer to the same bearers, even if they attach different descriptive information to those names, they may still communicate since their "reference remains the same."

A more sophisticated version of this line of thought can be drawn out of some remarks of Ludwig Wittgenstein (1889–1951). One goal of his *Philosophical Investigations* is to suggest a view of natural language as not needing to be measured against the standards of logically perfect languages such as those constructed by Frege. While such languages have a role to play in inquiry, natural languages function effectively for their human users not just in spite of, but in part *because of* the vagueness, open-endedness, and context sensitivity of the terms they contain. He writes,

> If one says, "Moses did not exist," this may mean various things. It may mean: the Israelites did not have a *single* leader when they withdrew from Egypt—or: their leader was not called Moses—or: there cannot have been anyone who accomplished all that the Bible relates of Moses, or: etc., etc. We may say, following Russell, the name "Moses" may be defined by various descriptions ... but when I make a statement about Moses,—am I always ready to substitute some *one* of these descriptions for "Moses"? Has the name "Moses" got a fixed and unequivocal use for me in all possible cases? (1958, pp. 36–37)

This point of view is further developed by Searle (1958). Searle denies that a proper name, even relative to an idiolect, is semantically equivalent to a set of descriptions. His reason is that if it were so equivalent, it would become superfluous (p. 171). It is not quite clear why superfluity would be a strike against a word: after all, acronyms are superfluous but still contribute to efficient communication. Nonetheless, Searle suggests that the practice of using proper names gains its utility by enabling us to refer to objects without our having to settle on a list of necessary and sufficient conditions an object must satisfy in order to be a name's bearer. He writes,

> But the uniqueness and immense pragmatic convenience of proper names in our language lie precisely in the fact that they enable us to refer publicly to objects without being forced to raise issues and come to agreement on what descriptive characteristics exactly constitute the identity of the object. They function not as descriptions, but as pegs on which to hang descriptions. Thus the looseness of the criteria

for proper names is a necessary condition for isolating the referring function from the describing function of language. (1958, p. 172)

It is in the nature of our practice of naming that we should not expect a name to be amenable to definition in terms of a precise set of descriptions. Nevertheless, Searle holds that each name is semantically associated with a "cluster" of descriptions at least some of which must be satisfied by its bearer:

> To put the same point differently, suppose we ask, "Why do we have proper names at all?" Obviously, to refer to individuals. "Yes, but descriptions could do that for us." But only at the cost of specifying identity conditions every time reference is made: suppose we agree to drop "Aristotle" and use, say, "the teacher of Alexander," then it is a necessary truth that the man referred to is Alexander's teacher—but it is a contingent fact that Aristotle ever went into pedagogy (though I am suggesting it is a necessary fact that Aristotle has the logical sum, inclusive disjunction, of properties commonly attributed to him: any individual not having at least some of these properties could not be Aristotle). (Searle 1958, p. 172)

What came to be known as the Cluster Theory of Names became a popular version of DTPN. Presumably, Searle would also accept the "co-reference" standard as all that is necessary for communication, so that even if two speakers use different descriptions from the same cluster associated with a name, they could communicate with each other so long as both descriptions apply uniquely to the same bearer.

In spite of the attractiveness of the Cluster version of DTPN, we do well to take a closer look at the final sentence from the second quotation from Searle. Imagine that when he was an infant, Aristotle's village found itself besieged by a Persian military operation that took him and his family into slavery. In this scenario, Aristotle grew up harvesting olives on a farm in Asia Minor and was given no opportunity to exercise his intellectual talents. As a result, he acquired none of the characteristics that any candidate group of properties would impute to him: he never taught Alexander the Great, was not a pupil of Plato, did not write about ethics, and so on. Given the clear if depressing possibility of such an alternative state of affairs, it would seem to follow that the properties that are normally associated with 'Aristotle' are at best true of him contingently. As a result, it is hard to see how the meaning of that name is captured by the aforementioned cluster of properties. Kripke, who formulated this objection to the Cluster Theory, draws the following conclusion:

> It is just not, in any intuitive sense of necessity, a necessary truth that Aristotle had the properties commonly attributed to him. … It would seem that it's a contingent fact that Aristotle ever did *any* of the things commonly attributed to him today, *any* of these great achievements that we so much admire. (Kripke 1980, p. 74)

Kripke's point is known as the "modal objection" to DTPN. It applies to the classical version as well as to its refinement as given by the Cluster approach. Another objection to DTPN is known as the "epistemic objection," which in turn has two aspects. The first of these observes that many speakers associate descriptive information with a name that does not single out its bearer uniquely. Consider the name 'Edgar G. Robinson.' Many people will know the name, but will associate with it such descriptive information as 'actor from the mid-twentieth century who usually played gangsters.' This, however, does not distinguish Edward G. Robinson from many others to whom it applies as well such as Sydney Greenstreet and James Cagney. Accordingly, even if a description does give the sense of a name, that description (at least as construed by the present version of the Descriptive Theory) will not pick out a unique bearer for many speakers.

The second aspect of the epistemic objection starts with the observation that many ordinary speakers are mistaken in the properties they associate with proper names. Ask an ordinary passerby on a city street who Einstein is, and she might tell you he invented the atom bomb; most likely, lots of folks believe Michelangelo painted *The Last Supper*, and so on. Yet such speakers nevertheless seem able to refer to these individuals by using their names. If, however, their associated descriptions were tasked with allowing their thoughts to pick out objects, many such thoughts would hit the wrong targets.

Particularly when we contemplate the modal objection to the Description Theory, we sense a view of names as somehow capturing a thing's essence. The reason is that much of what drives the foregoing example concerning Aristotle is the idea that *that very person* could have had different properties from those that he famously did have. This way of thinking of individuals is sometimes associated with the notion of *de re modality*: we pick out an individual and ask whether that very thing might have had different properties from those that it does in fact have. While some may jib at this way of thinking as being in some sense too metaphysical, we should note that it plays an important role in everyday thought and discourse. Imagine you've been accused of a crime. If in fact the accusation is correct, then the accusation very likely assumes that *you*—and not someone similar to but distinct from you such as your identical twin—could have done otherwise than commit the crime that you did. Likewise, if you are praised for a deed of bravery, that praise assumes that *you*—and not just some like you in certain respects—could instead have been less courageous and done something less praiseworthy than what you in fact did. Judges, juries, irate parents, and proud parents partake in some metaphysics, even if they don't notice the fact. This is not to say that we are prepared to answer all modal questions concerning an individual. While it seems clear that I, this very person, might have worn different socks from the ones that I am in fact wearing, and that I, this very person, could not have been an amoeba, it is difficult to know how to settle questions such as whether I could have been born in the Middle Ages, or could have become a successful musician (given that I have little musical talent). However, even if we acknowledge that there is a large swath of questions about de re modality that we do not know how to settle, we need not resolve them to accept the challenge to the Descriptive Theory.

A succinct way of putting the objection to DTPN is that most proper names are *rigid designators*, meaning that they have a constant intension: take any world you like, then they have the same extension in that world as they do in any other. On the rigid designation approach, most proper names of ordinary language refer to the same thing across all possible worlds in which that thing exists.[6] By contrast, the NPs that are normally used to elucidate the descriptive meaning of these names on behalf of DTPN are not rigid, but are instead what we might call flexible designators. That would seem to show that such descriptions cannot plausibly be used to elucidate the meaning of most proper names.

We seem now to find ourselves between a rock and a hard place. The Millian theory seems to face insurmountable objections; but now we see

---

6. I say "most" here because it is fairly clear that some proper names are used nonrigidly. 'Jack the Ripper' seems to be used to refer to whoever it is who is responsible for a series of brutal murders of prostitutes in late nineteenth-century London, and the name would evidently refer to different persons in different counterfactual situations.

that DTPN runs up against the rigidity of proper names. Before abandoning hope of progress, let us note that we may agree that ordinary proper names are rigid designators without yet relinquishing DTPN. The reason is that the rigidity of a proper name does not preclude its having a sense. Perhaps, instead, there are descriptions that themselves track the things that satisfy them across all possible worlds. Might there be, that is, rigid descriptive phrases? One suggestion is to let a name's meaning be given in terms of a person's genetic makeup. Such a makeup is arguably one that you have essentially, and so follows you through all possible situations in which you might have existed. On the other hand, that genetic makeup will be shared by identical twins, each of whom has a name that refers to him or her only. Further, we often name things that are not living creatures and so have no genetic makeup. Ships, nations, and freeways are cases in point. So appealing to genes here seems to be a dead end. What else might we try? We will return to this question in Section 4.5.

4.4. Direct Reference Returns, and Some Nihilism

It is not always fair to insist that a critic of a theory be able to provide an alternative that does at least as well as the one she had criticized. Instead, she might respond that she does not know where the truth lies, other than that the position she is criticizing is not going to work. Nonetheless, the most prominent critic of DTPN, Saul Kripke, did offer a sketch of an alternative approach which was subsequently developed and defended at some length by others. This alternative approach became known as a Causal Theory of Reference.

Before discussing that theory, let us recall that we are in this chapter focused only on characterization questions concerning linguistic meaning, and setting aside in-virtue-of-what questions. This point is easy to lose track of because as we shall see shortly, Kripke's notion of "fixing the reference" of a name, his use of the phrase "theory of reference," and his criticisms of certain forms of DTPN tend to obscure the distinction between characterization and in-virtue-of-what questions.

Kripke suggests that instead of supposing that a name homes in on an object by virtue of being semantically equivalent to a set of properties that together characterize that object uniquely, ordinary speakers manage to refer to things by using names that participate in a causal chain that in most cases traces back to an initial dubbing (1980, pp. 96-7). That dubbing, which might be achieved by such utterances as

"Let us call this baby 'Edward,'" will normally suffice to give the name a bearer. However, even if the dubbing ceremony uses descriptive information, that descriptive information need be no part of the name's meaning. Kripke uses the phrase "fixing the reference" in this connection, telling us that even if descriptive information is used to fix a name's reference, it need be no part of the name's semantic analysis. Nonetheless, a reference-fixing ceremony such as Kripke imagines might well imbue a word with meaning. In this limited respect, Kripke is offering a partial answer to the in-virtue-of-what question as it pertains to names. (It does not purport to be a complete answer, even for the case of names, since baptismal ceremonies will normally use words that have meaning prior to the occurrence of the ceremony.)

On the basis of his account of how descriptions may be used to help fix a name's reference without being carried over into that name's meaning, Kripke goes on to offer an account of how a user of a name that has already been introduced manages to refer to that name's bearer. If it cannot be by invoking a set of properties such as suggested by DTPN, what might it be instead? Kripke's answer is that it is instead by standing in a potentially very long series of causal connections that trace back to the introduction of the name.

> A rough statement of a theory might be the following: an initial "baptism" takes place. Here the object may be named by ostension, or the referent of the name may be fixed by description. When the name is "passed from link to link," the receiver of the name must, I think, intend when he learns it to use it with the same reference as the man from whom he heard it. (1980, p. 96)

I know the name 'Eddy Merckx' because I've seen it in print in cycling magazines, and perhaps also heard it used by announcers discussing races in which he made his mark on cycling. I can refer to the cyclist by using the name, not because I can articulate a set of descriptions that uniquely and rigidly apply to and only to Merckx; rather, I can refer to him by virtue of standing in a causal chain in which I use the name with the intention that it refer to whoever was being referred to by the person or persons that I acquired the name from. This account is not meant to make our practice of naming any less confusing than it already often is: historians sometimes come across names about whom there is some question whether they have bearers at all; likewise, baby-switching, intentional or not, can result in our using a name to refer to what we think is one child when in fact it is another. The Causal Theory is not meant to solve such problems, but rather to describe the practice as it is, warts and all.

The Causal Theory of Reference is not offering an answer to the characterization question. Further, it is offering only a partial answer to the in-virtue-of-what question in that it offers to account for how proper names come to have the meanings that they do. That answer is not likely to turn into a complete account of in virtue of what words have meaning, however, since it presupposes that we already have descriptive phrases with which to carry out name introductions. At the same time, others have been inspired by the arguments of *Naming and Necessity* to look anew at the arguments that were thought to undermine Direct Reference. Recall that certain of these arguments turned on our judgments about differential truth values for sentences that are alike except for one name. (One such sentence contains 'Superman,' for instance, while the other contains 'Clark Kent'; they are otherwise just alike.) But we also have independent reason to think that ordinary speakers tend to run together the question of a sentence's truth with other factors which we may now term pragmatic. For instance, the following dialogue seems perfectly intelligible:

> 4.13. A. Remember Elijah and Sidney from high school? Well, they fell in love and got married.
>
>   B. That's not what I heard. I heard they got married and fell in love.

From what we've learned about the logical properties of 'and,' we have reason to think that a sentence of the form 'P & Q' has just the same truth conditions as 'Q & P.' However, this dialogue suggests that a speaker who asserts a sentence of the form 'P and Q,' where the two conjuncts refer to dateable events, is often understood as suggesting that these two events occurred in the order in which they are mentioned. Such a suggestion is no part of the utterance's truth conditions, however, any more than that it is part of the truth conditions of a sentence containing the phrase 'spring chicken' that it refers to someone who is elderly.

We cannot blame speakers for failing to draw all the distinctions that we find useful for analytical purposes in the Philosophy of Language. Instead, we may draw from 4.13 the moral that everyday speakers do not always recognize such distinctions, and furthermore that our own intuitions about cases that challenged Direct Reference might have been influenced by those everyday judgments. Perhaps when we use a particular name to ascribe an attitude to someone, we are only suggesting, rather than strictly committing ourselves to, the claim that she would accept that ascription. Accordingly, when we say for instance,

4.14. Lois Lane thinks that Clark Kent is a reporter.

We rightly suggest, but only suggest, that she would agree with that ascription so worded. But we can also truly say such things as:

4.15. Superman sure has everyone tricked. Even Lois Lane thinks Superman is a mild-mannered reporter![7]

4.15 may be true even if it is clear that Lois is ignorant of Superman's identity. More generally, the so-called pragmatic defense of Direct Reference attempts to defuse the examples seeming to undermine it by showing that their force rests on a subtle conflation of semantic content with pragmatic implication.[8]

Before proceeding it will be useful to pause to consider two minority views about the semantics of proper names. According to one of these views, defended for instance in Ziff (1960), proper names have no meaning at all, but are instead governed by customs and patterns of usage only. As evidence for this view, note that some dictionaries do not have entries for names, and it does seem as if one can know a language without knowing the names by which people and things are customarily called. Further, it might be held that our sense of the autonomy of the naming relation might be due to the fact that many of us live in societies that enforce penal, tax, contract, and other kinds of regime that necessitate the ossification of such customs: government officials find it convenient to track individuals by a name so that they can hold them accountable for misdeeds, taxes owed, contracts to one another, and service to the state. Our sense that an individual may be correctly or incorrectly referred to by a particular name may be just an artifact of particular political configurations.

According to a less extreme type of nihilism, a proper name has a meaning, but not in a way that can be characterized by relating it to a particular object. Instead, proper names function like so-called

---

7. This example is inspired by Berg (1988).
8. Salmon (1986) and Soames (2002) are prominent works that develop that strategy in different ways.

indexical expressions (discussed in more detail in Chapter 5), which only refer to objects relative to a context of utterance. In current parlance, names have a linguistic meaning (and in particular what in the next chapter we will call a 'character') that determines their intension only after a context of utterance has been fixed. The word 'I' does not have a fixed bearer. Rather, it refers to whomever is using it in a given utterance event. Similarly, 'you' refers to the addressee (if there is one) of such an utterance event, and so on for many other expressions such as 'he,' 'we,' 'yesterday,' and 'now.' The modestly nihilistic view of names will suggest that names like 'Michael' and 'Priyanka' are not so different from these other words: the latter is to be used to refer (and these are defeasible norms) to whomever is the most salient female who customarily has been so-called in recent episodes of reference, while the former is used in a similar way except for males. Might this approach provide a reasonable compromise between Direct Reference and Millianism?

4.5. The New Fregeans

The criticisms leveled against DTPN that we considered in Section 4.3 raised the question whether some other version of that theory might be defensible. We toyed with the idea that names carry genetic information, but that suggestion did not seem promising. Might there be a way of finding descriptions that (a) rigidly track their bearers where appropriate, (b) apply to a sufficiently wide range of names, and (c) are plausibly things that everyday speakers know by virtue of knowing someone's or something's name?

Here is a suggestion going at least as far back as W. Kneale (1962): perhaps we could characterize the meaning of name N as 'the thing that bears name 'N.'' After all, one thing that we can all be confident of is that Eddy Merckx is called 'Eddy Merckx,' at least in English. A similar pattern would seem to apply for anything that has a name. So we seem to be meeting desiderata (b) and (c). Our first desideratum, however, would seem to be a problem. For surely that very person, Eddy Merckx, might not have borne that name: just as we can imagine a situation in which Aristotle never had an opportunity to reflect on courage and justice, so, too, it would seem that we can easily imagine a possible situation in which Eddy Merckx bears some other name.

This problem, however, would seem to be tractable. As background, one approach to the meaning of the word 'actually' is that it rigidly refers to the possible world in which it is uttered. To see this, consider the difference between

> The actual winner of the race might not have worn socks.
> The winner of the race might not have worn socks.

Suppose that George won the race. Then the first sentence says that George might not have worn socks, whether or not he won the race. On the other hand, the second makes no specific reference to George. It would be true in a situation in which Susan both wins the race and rides sockless. Likewise, the phrase 'the actual bearer of the name "Eddy Merckx"' always refers back to the person who in the actual world bears that name. But if that is so, then we have found a way of "rigidifying" a description, while still meeting desiderata (b) and (c).

This revision of DTPN has, however, been harshly criticized. Kripke famously attacks it as being circular. Imagining a characterization of the meaning of 'Socrates' as "The man named 'Socrates'," Kripke writes,

> As a theory of the reference of the name "Socrates" it will lead immediately to a vicious circle. If one was determining the referent of a name like "Glunk" to himself and made the following decision, "I shall use the term 'Glunk' to refer to the man that I call 'Glunk'," this would get one nowhere. One had better have some independent determination of the referent of "Glunk." This is a good example of blatantly circular determination. (1980, p. 73)

We noted earlier that Kripke uses the term "theory of reference" in a way that goes beyond a pure semantic characterization. Rather, as he uses the term, he appears to have in mind a theory that will also explain how our names come to have the meaning they do, that is, as an at least partial answer to the in-virtue-of-what question. However, if we restrict our aspirations to that of characterization only, this objection need not perturb us.

In hindsight, it appears that Kripke is subtly shifting the standard of evaluation of the DTPN from one on which it is supposed to characterize the linguistic meaning of proper names, to one on which it is supposed to answer the in-virtue-of-what question. However, one can offer DTPN while renouncing any aspiration to answer the latter question and instead treat it as giving a semantic characterization only. True, that semantic characterization cannot teach a speaker a name's meaning if she does not know it already, but it may nevertheless be used to capture what a competent user of a name knows when she does know its meaning.

Another question we might raise about Kneale's proposal as modified here concerns the fact that many people share a name. Two approaches present themselves. One is that all such cases involve homonymy: two people who are both called 'Susan Entwhistle' have names that are spelled and pronounced just alike, even though these are different words. (In this respect the situation would be similar to the way in which 'bat' can be used to mean either a type of flying mammal, or an implement used in baseball.)[9] Another approach would suggest that a name shares properties with certain pronouns like 'here' and 'I.' As we shall see in more detail in Chapter 5, many current theories of these terms will hold that what they refer to on a given occasion is determined in part by their linguistic meaning, but also by the context in which they're used. George's use of 'I' refers to him, while Virginia's use of 'I' refers to her. Perhaps proper names have an implicitly context-sensitive dimension as well, so that usually context enables us to determine which Susan Entwhistle is being referred to by that name. (And when it does not, we can ask for clarification with a question such as "Which 'Susan Entwhistle' are you talking about?")

4.6. Study Questions and Suggestions for Further Reading

Study Questions

1. Please explain how DTPN can capture the distinctive a priori and a posteriori status of certain identity statements (such as 4.6 and 4.7).
2. Please use the concept of possible worlds to explain what it would mean for a sentence to be necessarily true, as well as what it would mean for a sentence to be necessarily false.
3. Please give an example of a predicate whose extension is not empty, and which has the same extension in all possible worlds.
4. If you have read Evans (1973), please discuss whether the Causal Theory of Reference could be modified in such a way as to accommodate Evans's example involving Madagascar.

---

9. Recent scholarship has also seen a growing interest in *predicativism* about names, according to which names are fundamentally count nouns. Thus 'John is laughing' will be analyzed as 'The John is laughing.' Because there are many Johns, we then apply the tools developed for understanding incomplete definite descriptions to assign plausible truth conditions to the quoted sentence. See Bach (2015) for fuller discussion.

5. Kripke (1980) argues that some sentences are necessarily true in spite of being a posteriori. Please explain his reasons for that conclusion. Do you find them compelling? Please explain your answer.

Further Reading (with recommended [*] items for instructors)

The passage from Mill (1843)* pertinent to the semantics of names is brief and accessible. Cumming (2019) is a linguistically and philosophically informed discussion of names. Textor (2011) and Heck and May (2006) are both excellent introductions to Frege's discussion of sense and reference. Wittgenstein (1958) and Searle (1958) provide classic formulations of the "Cluster Theory" of proper names. Kripke* (1980) is the groundbreaking work challenging the hegemony of the Descriptive Theory, althouth it is now widely acknowledged that R. Marcus anticipated many of his insights; see for instance Marcus (1961). Evans (1973)* provides a lucid and compelling counterexample to Kripke's Causal Theory of Reference. Berg (1988), Salmon (1986), and Soames (2002) provide different types of defense of Direct Reference on pragmatic grounds, and Recanati (1993) provides partial defense of that view. Green (1998) challenges aspects of Salmon (1986) and Recanati (1993). Geurts (1997) responds to Kripke's criticisms of Kneale and defends an updated version of the latter's theory of proper names. Bach (2015) expounds the view, which is a development of Kneale's, known as *predicativism* about names.

References

Bach, K. 2015. "The Predicate View of Proper Names." *Philosophy Compass* 10: 772–784.

Berg, J. 1988. "The Pragmatics of Substitutivity." *Linguistics and Philosophy* 11: 355–370.

Cumming, S. 2019. "Names." In *Stanford Encyclopedia of Philosophy*, edited by Edward Zalta. https://plato.stanford.edu/

Evans, G. 1973. "The Causal Theory of Names." *Proceedings of the Aristotelian Society* 47: 187–208.

Frege, G. (1892) 1970. "On Sense and Reference." In *Translations from the Philosophical Writings of Gottlob Frege*, edited by P. Geach and M. Black and translated by M. Black, 56–78. Oxford: Basil Blackwell.

Geurts, B. 1997. "Good News about the Description Theory of Names." *Journal of Semantics* 14: 319–348.

Green, M. 1998. "Direct Reference and Implicature." *Philosophical Studies* 91: 61–90.

Heck, R., and May, R. 2006. "Frege's Contribution to Philosophy of Language." In *The Oxford Handbook of Philosophy of Language*, edited by E. Lepore and B. Smith, 3–39. Oxford: Oxford University Press.

Kneale, W. 1962. "Modality De Dicto and De Re." In *Logic, Methodology, and Philosophy of Science. Proceedings of the 1960 International Congress*, edited by E. Nagel, P. Suppes, and A. Tarski, 622–633. Stanford, CA: Stanford University Press.

Kripke, S. 1980. *Naming and Necessity*. Cambridge, MA: Harvard University Press.

Marcus, R. 1961. "Modalities and Intensional Languages." *Synthese* 13: 303–322.

Mill, J. S. (1843) 2011. *A System of Logic*. Cambridge: Cambridge University Press.

Putnam, H. 1996. "The Meaning of Meaning." In *The Twin Earth Chronicles*, edited by S. Goldberg and A. Pessin (Oxford: Routledge), pp. 3–52.

Recanati, F. 1993. *Direct Reference: From Language to Thought*. Cambridge, Mass: Wiley-Blackwell.

Ryle, G. 1949. "Meaning and Necessity." *Philosophy* 24: 67–76.

Salmon, N. 1986. *Frege's Puzzle*. Cambridge, MA: MIT Press.

Searle, J. 1958. "Proper Names." *Mind* 67: 166–173.

Soames, S. 2002. *Beyond Rigidity: The Unfinished Semantic Agenda of Naming and Necessity*. Oxford: Oxford University Press.

Textor, M. 2011. *Frege on Sense and Reference*. London: Routledge.

Wittgenstein, L. 1958. *Philosophical Investigations*. Translated by G. E. M. Anscombe. London: Macmillan.

Ziff, P. 1960. *Semantic Analysis*. Ithaca, NY: Cornell University Press.

CHAPTER 5

Speech Acts and Conversations

Chapter Overview

This chapter discusses a concept bequeathed by a breakaway movement that developed in the middle of the twentieth century known as Ordinary Language Philosophy (OLP). OLP denied that human languages can be fully understood with the tools of formal logic, and it focused instead on the subtle ways in which speakers' situations can determine what they say, as well as much communicative content going beyond what they say. OLP also made revolutionary claims about how to resolve ancient philosophical problems. Though few of these claims have been substantiated, an enduring legacy of that movement is the concept of a speech act, or illocutionary act, which has emerged as a focus of research in recent years.

5.1. Locution, Illocution, Perlocution

By the middle of the twentieth century, Anglophone philosophy had come to take seriously the task of making progress on traditional philosophical problems through analysis of the language in which those problems are expressed. However, by that time there had also arisen a division between two camps within this movement, sometimes called the *formalists* and *informalists*. The former we have in effect discussed in the last two chapters. Discerning an intimate connection between meaning and truth conditions, formalists were hard at work developing sophisticated semantic theories of various regions of language, most notably those regions involved in science and mathematics. However, a rogue faction, which came to be known as the Ordinary Language movement, broke with this tradition and was now preparing to challenge it.

We may appreciate OLP in light of an example aimed at challenging the truth-conditional hegemony. To that end, let's return to Russell's analysis of definite descriptions as discussed in Chapter 3. You will remember that according to Russell, a sentence such as 'The current Queen of Iceland is rich,' when uttered at a moment at which Iceland is not a monarchy, is perfectly meaningful (since it has a definite set of truth conditions), but false (the actual world is not a member of that set of conditions). Strawson (1950) objects that calling this sentence "false" does not comport with everyday linguistic practice. His reason is that if you were in the year 2020 to approach a stranger and remark, "The current Queen of Iceland is rich," she would probably not reply that what you said was false; rather, she would more likely rejoin with something like "Sorry, you're a bit confused. Iceland is a parliamentary republic." Strawson observes as well that the stranger might also reply that the question of the sentence's truth does not even arise. Many have taken this to be a direct attack on Russell's account of the meaning of descriptive sentences. (We will see later that it is not so clear that it is a direct attack on it.)

Strawson's point highlights what has come to be known as *presupposition-failure*. We'll consider more precise definitions in Chapter 6, but for now, let us say that a presupposition is any assumption that we take for granted when we speak to others or reason on our own. Some words or expressions seem particularly apt for making clear what we are presupposing in our utterances. Consider, for instance,

5.1. Even Henry can play bridge.

Someone who utters 5.1 will normally be heard as taking for granted that if anyone might be expected to have trouble playing bridge, it will be Henry. So, too, recalling our it-cleft example from Chapter 3:

3.24. It was John who ate all the cookies.

Here we would expect the speaker to be taking for granted that all parties to her utterance are already aware that someone ate all the cookies, and they have at least some interest in finding the culprit. Linguists and philosophers have spent considerable effort on identifying and codifying those expressions in the world's languages that "trigger" presuppositions.

Strawson's charge against Russell, at least as it has been most commonly understood, is that when a sentence exhibits presupposition failure, then rather than being false, that sentence is *neither true nor false*. (Strawson himself reinforces this interpretation of his earlier criticism in his 1952, pp. 175–179.) The idea of a sentence being neither true nor false is not as exotic as it may at first appear. For instance, consider the sentence "It weighs 11 kilos," spoken in a situation in which nothing is around that might plausibly be being talked about—no anvils, encyclopedias, or bulldogs. Grammarians would consider this a sentence, and yet in a situation in which neither the speaker nor her addressees has any idea what the 'it' is that the sentence refers to, the sentence is apparently neither true nor false. Some philosophers like to describe sentences that are neither true nor false as exhibiting "truth-value gaps."

For decades after Strawson's famous critique of Russell, philosophers and linguists put great effort into developing formal techniques for the accommodation of the former's semantic notion of presupposition. This work shed light on the phenomenon of presupposition, but the posit of truth-value gaps was not mandated by the linguistic data that Strawson isolated. Instead, another option inviting exploration was the possibility of an *illocutionary misfire*. It will take a bit of work to build up to that notion, which we will explain in Section 5.4. Before doing so we need to understand the notion of an illocutionary act.

In his classic work *How to Do Things with Words* (1962), Austin sets out to challenge a then-widespread dogma about the function of language:

Descriptive Dogma: the primary or central function of language is to describe the world.[1]

Austin knows that it is widely agreed that language can be used for other purposes beside description: few would deny that language can be used

---

1. Austin calls this the "Descriptive fallacy," but we will not adopt that terminology here. The reason is that as we are using the term, "fallacy" only applies to certain lines of reasoning. On this usage, it therefore makes no sense to call a proposition or claim a fallacy.

to order, insult, or spin a yarn. On the other hand, a long philosophical tradition holds that these other uses are secondary, parasitic, or in some other way not quite up to a standard meriting philosophical attention. Instead, according to the Descriptive Dogma, a paradigm use of language is in such a sentence as:

> 5.2. Air in the earth's atmosphere is composed primarily of nitrogen, oxygen, argon, carbon dioxide, and water vapor.

5.2 is, Austin will agree, a perfectly good sentence that conveys information that took considerable effort to ascertain. However, he will challenge the Descriptive Dogma by pointing out that many of the things we do with language other than describing the world are of cognitive, social, and ethical significance, and that we have no good reason for relegating them to secondary status compared to that of description.

To appreciate Austin's position, let us note first some of the potentially far-reaching things we do with words other than describing (or merely describing) the world. Imagine such utterances as the following made in the scenarios indicated:

> 5.3. The meeting is adjourned (as spoken by the committee chair).
> 5.4. The court finds you guilty of voluntary manslaughter (as uttered by the presiding judge in a courtroom).
> 5.5. I bet $10,000 on Equus to place (as uttered by a gambler at a racetrack).

Each of these is an indicative sentence, but as uttered under the conditions suggested by the parenthetical comment appended to it, it will have potentially momentous consequences. 5.5 puts the speaker at risk of losing a substantial sum of money, and; 5.4 puts the defendant being addressed at risk of incarceration. 5.3 might have the implication that a person attending that meeting will lose the opportunity to challenge a committee's finding. Perhaps he had applied for a license to open a restaurant in a certain location, and now has been barred from doing so.

The aforementioned three are all examples of what Austin would have called *doing things with words*, but where the doing is more than just an utterance. Such doings have social significance reaching well beyond the mere fact of the utterance itself. One way to highlight that significance is to make it explicit in what one says. To see how this works, note that we can sometimes do something by saying that we are doing so. Alas, I cannot learn Swahili by saying, "I hereby learn Swahili." The most I can do with these or similar words is commit myself to the project of learning it; and that project may take years to complete. On the other hand, in many cases I can make a promise by saying (or writing, possibly in the presence of a Notary Public) that I am doing so, as in, "I promise to pay off your loan if you're unable to do so." Likewise, if I have the required religious and legal authority, and a couple have said their vows and met any other needed conditions, I can make that pair into a married couple by saying, "I now pronounce you wife and wife." Utterances in which one describes oneself as performing a certain act, and, in so doing, also performs that act, are commonly known as *performatives*. A terse way of putting Austin's insight is with the idea that in some instances, *saying can make it so*.

Austin would acknowledge that these cases of performatives are relatively uncommon. Instead, for the most part we perform significant acts in speaking but without describing ourselves as performing those acts. However, even in such cases we could make explicit what we are doing. Suppose then that the following sentence is uttered as a statement of fact:

5.6. It's starting to snow outside.

The speaker is making an assertion. It is therefore similar to

5.7. I assert that it's starting to snow outside.

5.7 is a bit more pedantic than 5.6, but it will play largely the same function. We may think of the second one as indicating the way in which the first one was meant. We'll return to this point shortly.

More generally, except for utterances such as those in which we are checking to see if our vocal chords are working as we recover from laryngitis, or testing a microphone on the sound system for the concert we're about to give, there is a further question of how we mean that utterance. To illustrate, suppose my student arrives late to class for the third time this week. I say to him,

5.8. You'll be more punctual in the future.

It's pretty clear *what* I am saying, and as we now know from Chapter 3, this "content" can be expressed as a function from possible worlds to the set {T, F}. However, this leaves unanswered the question whether I mean what I say as a prediction or instead as a warning. These different aspects of how a single content may be meant have come to be known as different kinds of *illocutionary force*.

With the aim of elucidating the notion of force, Austin offers a tripartite distinction among three types of act:

> *Locutionary act*: an act of uttering a meaningful phrase or sentence. (This is equivalent to our notion of saying$_{thin}$ from chapter 2.)
>
> *Illocutionary act*: an act of a sort that can (though need not) be performed by saying and speaker-meaning that one is doing so. (This is equivalent to our notion of saying$_{thick}$ from previous chapters.)
>
> *Perlocutionary act*: a characteristic consequence of an illocutionary act.

All illocutionary acts are characterized by having at least one illocutionary force. (We will consider later the possibility that some have more than one force.) Such acts are normally but not always performed by means of a locutionary act. In addition, such acts have characteristic, but not exceptionless consequences on, for instance, the psychological states of addressees. Further, we have just seen that knowing what locutionary act has been performed does not enable us to deduce what illocutionary act has been. This may be expressed as the thought that locutionary content underdetermines illocutionary force: a single sentence, expressing the same content from one tokening to another, might be used as a prediction in one tokening, a warning in another, and a guess in yet another. These various uses are different ways in which that content may be speaker-meant.

This way of thinking about the agentive dimension of speech acts brings out some distinctions that are otherwise difficult to discern. For instance, with the help of Austin's tripartition, we may see that telling you something and convincing you of something are quite different acts. I can "hereby" tell you that it's time to leave the party or that I am going to support your candidacy in the upcoming election. However, I can't "hereby" convince you of anything unless I have an unusual power over your mind. Instead, whether you are convinced or not is up to you, and at most indirectly under my control. Stretching the notion of act a bit, Austin will say that in such a situation, if you do find my words persuasive, then I have performed the perlocutionary act of convincing you.

Another theme emerging from Austin's discussion of speech act is their conventional nature. We saw in Chapter 1 that the current consensus about linguistic meaning holds that it is determined by conventions: words mean what they do not by virtue of an inherent resemblance between themselves and what they represent, for instance, but by virtue of their being conventionally used to represent the things that they do. These are semantic conventions securing what our words literally mean.

Austin goes beyond the consensus about semantic conventions to claim that there are also conventions enabling us to perform illocutionary acts. Such extra-semantic conventions would seem to enable a speaker to illocute by making a particular utterance under appropriate conditions. Conventions govern a wide range of behaviors. For instance, kicking a ball through some goal posts under certain conditions counts as a field goal in American football, while sticking your tongue out at another person in traditional Tibetan culture counts as a polite greeting. Austin's student J. Searle (1969) has conjectured that a similar pattern may be discerned in many speech acts. For instance, it would seem that one way to appoint someone to a professional post is for an authorized person to say such words as "I hereby appoint you to the post of treasurer," or something of the kind.

Similarly, one way to articulate a conventionalist approach to speech acts is with the formula,

Saying X, in situation Z, counts as doing Y.

Here "counting as" is intended to suggest an analogy with the way in which, for example, kicking a ball into a certain net under certain circumstances counts as scoring a goal in soccer.

Austin's remarks suggest that he holds that all illocutionary acts are made possible by extra-semantic conventions (1962, p. 105). This position is controversial: while we might agree that some illocutionary acts may be so described, it seems to be going too far to hold that all such acts are. Consider the act of refusing: one can refuse by saying that one is doing so: one might say, "I refuse to let you pass," to someone who is trying to get through a passageway that you control. On the other hand, one might just stand in that passageway in such an attitude as to make clear that you have no intention of letting the other party through. Here it doubtful that such a case of refusing to let someone pass relies on conventions.

How else might we explain how the person in the passageway refuses passage to others without invoking extra-semantic conventions? One approach is that by standing as he does, he *intentionally manifests his intention* to disallow passage. We might imagine him with a stern face, arms crossed over his chest, beady stare, and so on; all these are ways of indicating that he will be preventing others from getting through, and others can readily discern this. What is more, and in light of our discussion of expression in Chapter 2, if he does this with the intention of manifesting these intentions, he is also *expressing* his intention. Here, then, we have a way of understanding a speech act that does not require appealing to conventions.

In a landmark paper, Strawson (1964) argued that Austin overgeneralized from certain cases to conclude that all speech acts are dependent upon extra-semantic conventions.

> I do not want to deny that there may be conventional postures or procedures for entreating: one can, for example, kneel down, raise one's arms, and say, "I entreat you." But I do want to deny that an act of entreaty can be performed only as conforming to such conventions. …[T]o suppose that there is always and necessarily a convention conformed to would be like supposing that there could be no love affairs which did not proceed on lines laid down in the *Roman de la Rose* or that every dispute between men must follow the pattern specified in Touchstone's speech about the countercheck quarrelsome and the lie direct. (1964, p. 444)

Strawson concedes that some speech acts depend upon extra-semantic conventions, but he doubts that this holds across the board. What, however, could make a locutionary into an illocutionary act save the invocation of a convention? Strawson's answer is that intentions rather than conventions may do the needed work here, and to appreciate his approach we do well to consider the notion of speaker meaning, the topic of the next section.

5.2. Speaker Meaning

Let's return to the "saying makes it so" feature of performatives. On closer inspection, this turns out to be a slippery criterion, not least because 'say' is used in many ways in everyday discourse. Among the two ways that most interest us here are those in which the speaker means what she says, and those in which she does not do so. I might, in rehearsing my lines for my upcoming Shakespeare performance say,

> Alas, poor Yorick. I knew him, Horatio, a fellow of infinite jest, of most excellent fancy.

As it happens, I have never known anyone named Yorick, jester or otherwise. Further, if someone were to hear me rehearse this line, in full awareness that I am only rehearsing lines for a play, she would have no basis for accusing me of being a liar. Likewise, people who are speaking ironically often find it necessary to clarify to others that they did not mean what they said.

In his important article, "Meaning" (Grice 1957), Grice noted that common sense makes use of two distinct notions of meaning. One of these is "natural meaning," exemplified in such utterances as "These skid marks mean that the car was speeding when it turned the corner." This kind of meaning, as we noted in Chapter 1, is not particularly germane to communication, not least because it would seem that every item in the universe conveys information of some kind and thus is a bearer of natural meaning in some sense. By contrast, Grice draws our attention to such remarks as

> In putting on her coat, Wallace meant it was time for us to leave the party.

(Imagine Wallace puts on her coat in plain view of her friends, perhaps even staring at them beadily as she does so.) Wallace's behavior as thus described seems germane to communication even though she does not use language. What is more, Grice offers an account of the conditions required to make such a sentence true. Just putting on a coat is not by itself sufficient to mean anything in this sense of 'mean,' since a person might put on a coat in preparing to go outdoors with no intention of sending any message to anyone else. In fact, she might put on a coat with an intention of getting others to think she is going outside without meaning any such thing. Here is why. Perhaps she knows she is being watched by someone trying to spy on her, and she puts on her coat intending to get him to think she is going outside (perhaps to throw him off her trail). Even in this case she does not mean that she is going outdoors. Instead, meaning of a sort germane to communication seems to require not just intending to convey information, but also intending to convey it in a way that makes that very intention available to view. "Available to view," note, does not require that the intention is in fact "viewed": one might mean something in making an utterance, but not be heard because an ambulance passes by at just that moment, drowning out one's voice.

With this communicative notion of meaning in hand, we may now observe that an actor who utters the Shakespeare sentence "Alas, poor Yorick ... ," says it without meaning it. (He could still say it with feeling, and indeed play the part convincingly.) By contrast, in a speech act, the agent must speaker-mean what she says, whether it be as an assertion, a promise, a command, a question, or some other speech act. Accordingly, we may characterize a speech act as an *act of a type that an agent can, but need not, carry out by saying and speaker-meaning that she is doing so.* As before, however, just as one can throw a ball without saying that one is doing so, one can assert, accept, or command, without saying that one is doing so.

We now have the pieces needed for understanding how to illocute without invoking extra-sematic conventions. We may do so by noting that speakers have the means at their disposal to manifest their intentions to undertake a variety of commitments: facial expression, tone of voice, gesture, all enable us to do so. Words do as well: by describing myself as, say, claiming that P, I can undertake a commitment to P as a claim (rather than with some other force), and thereby claim that P. Observe here that we are invoking semantic conventions and intentions, but no conventions that go beyond those that give our words their semantic properties. As such we have supported Strawson's challenge to Austin's view that all speech acts depend on extra-semantic conventions for their realization.

5.3. Varieties of Speech Acts and Conversations

In illocutionary acts we have unearthed a dimension of language use that is not captured or encoded by sentences, phrases, or their semantic values. It is natural to wonder next about the contours of this dimension. Can speech acts be put into any useful taxonomy like biological species, or are they more like clouds, where we can draw some very general distinctions (as we do between cirrus, stratus, and nimbus clouds, for instance) but where we still expect to encounter great variety and few clear boundaries from one case to the next? Austin thought he could distinguish among five categories of speech act which he termed verdictives, exercitives, commissives, behabitives, and expositives, roughly characterized and illustrated in Table 5.1. (Notice that in each case listed, one can perform the act named by describing oneself as doing so.)

While Austin's taxonomy is a good start, one might wish for some principles to guide us in determining a rationale for any taxonomy. After all, while behabitives are characterized in terms of attitudes and social behavior, would not those characteristics apply equally well to

TABLE 5.1 Austin's Five Types of Illocutionary Act

Illocutionary act type	Function	Examples
Verdictives	To render a verdict	Acquit, diagnose, grade, find
Exercitives	To exercise power, rights or influence	Appoint, order, pardon, resign
Commissives	To commit oneself to a course of action	Promise, agree
Behabitives	Concern attitudes and "social behavior"	Apologize, thank, welcome, curse
Expositives	Explain how our utterances fit into a larger conversation	Define, identify, conjecture, class

exercitives? Similarly, Table 5.1 gives us no reason to expect that the five types of speech act are exhaustive of the possible kinds, or instead simply describe those that Austin happened to notice in his particular social, linguistic, and historical milieu. Would we find a different taxonomy if we were to investigate speech act types in Swahili or Urdu?

Austin's student John Searle attempted to answer these questions in the mid-1960s with a new approach. He begins by delineating some basic concepts for understanding speech acts. One such concept is that of *direction of fit*, a notion pertaining to what we are trying to attain in our thought and speech. To take a famous example, suppose that A goes to the grocery store with a list of items to purchase.[2] A's job is to make sure that upon checking out, his cart contains all and only the items on that list. Accordingly, the world (at least as it is found in A's cart) is supposed to conform to what is on his list. Now suppose further that B, a private investigator, has been hired to find out what A has been buying. (Suppose A is suspected of insurance fraud.) B will also produce a list of grocery items, and he aims to ensure that his list matches precisely what is in A's cart. However, B's list has a different function from A's, for B's list is supposed to match the contents of the cart. If there is a disparity between B's list and what's in the cart, B cannot rectify it by changing the cart's contents. Instead, he has to revise the list.

A natural conclusion to draw from the supermarket vignette is that there are at least two kinds of direction of fit: word-to-world and

---

2. The example is derived with modifications from Anscombe (1957).

world-to-word. Linguistic tokens with the former direction of fit are in some appropriate sense supposed to match up to the world, while linguistic tokens with the latter direction of fit are supposed to get the world to match up to them. The distinction applies not just to lists, but to sentences as well, and it is here that we find a potential new foundation for the theory of speech acts. For it would seem that a deep distinction between types of utterance is between those, such as assertions, that aim to describe how things are, and those, such as imperatives, that aim to get others to behave in a certain manner. Questions might be construed in this framework as proposals that some subset (not necessarily proper) of conversationalists ascertain or provide information, namely the information that would answer the question. As such, the posing of a question may be a suggestion paraphrased as "Let's find out whether/who/where, etc."

Having one rather than another direction of fit is not enough to determine a unique illocutionary force, for two utterances might have the same direction of fit while differing in force. Consider the difference between an assertion and a guess. Both aim accurately to characterize the world. However, they differ in important respects: if A asserts that there will be thunderstorms tomorrow, then she is offering to inform us of some fact, and if we are all skeptical of her claim, we're within our rights to ask, "How do you know that?"[3] Alternatively, if she only guesses that there will be thunderstorms tomorrow, she is not offering to inform us, and the how-do-you-know question would not be appropriate. (She could justifiably reply, "Hey, it was just a guess!")

Searle (1979a) develops an account of the range of possible illocutionary forces rather than just those that are mentioned or employed in a particular language. To do this, he offers an account of each possible force as being fully characterized by twelve distinct parameters. On this approach, we know all there is to know about a given force by knowing where it lies along each of those twelve parameters. We have already seen one such parameter, namely direction of fit. Other parameters include what Searle calls illocutionary point (the ostensible aim of the speech act, such as to produce belief, or to produce action), the expressed psychological state (some speech acts express belief, while

---

3. This point relating assertion to knowledge is made by Williamson (1996).

others express intention, for instance), and the degree of strength of the act in question (such as the difference between asserting and guessing).

Searle offers other features characterizing illocutionary force which we do not need to dwell upon here. Instead, we might at this point wonder how speech acts so characterized fit into the larger conversations in which they normally occur. While it does sometimes happen that a passerby makes a one-off comment ("You dropped your scarf!") that might generate no more than an appreciative nod from you, many other speech acts are embedded in conversations. Further, many speech acts seem purpose-built to go with others. A question about what is the case, for instance, calls for an answer, which interlocutors aim to arrive at by pooling their information. By contrast, a question about what to do (how we can make it to the 9 p.m. movie on time, or how to keep the eggs we're cooking from sticking to the pan) often involves pooling our practical knowledge, much of which will be arrived at by trial and error. As these examples suggest, conversations are not disjointed series of speech acts like items on a shopping list. Instead, they tend to have something like a *telos*, or aim that interlocutors are striving to achieve: we want to find ingredients for the recipe we are making, or what time doors open at the club where our favorite band is performing, or what might happen if we. ... Such aims are not just ones that all participants in the conversation happen to share. Instead, they not only share those aims, but mutually acknowledge that they share them.

This line of thought suggests an idea that has come to be of central importance in recent philosophy of language and linguistics, namely that of common ground (or CG in what follows). To understand this notion, start out with the idea of an agent *accepting* a proposition, whether that acceptance be in the form of belief, presumption as true, or even as a guess or supposition for the sake of argument. Two people might accept that P without being aware that they both do so. However, if they both come to realize that they both accept P, then P becomes part of CG. One symptom of a proposition's being part of CG among a group of speakers is that it can be overtly taken for granted, for instance in their speech. Suppose we are walking outside, and as we do so a strong wind breaks a branch off a tree; the branch now comes crashing down, narrowly missing us both. I now remark,

Well *that* was a close call!

In speaking as I do, I am treating it as CG among us that what I am referring to could have caused harm.[4] As we will see in Chapter 6, CG plays a central role in clarifying how context is exploited to good effect in everyday discourse.

Back to conversations: What kinds of goals might interlocutors share and work toward achieving? Among the most common such aims are (i) gathering information, which we may construe as finding an answer to a question about what is the case (known as a theoretical question), and (ii) settling on a course of action, which might require different contributions from different parties, such as usually occurs when people play music together. Settling on a course of action may also be described as answering a practical question.

In light of our discussion thus far, let us say that whereas a *verbal exchange* is any sequence of speech acts, a *conversation* is a sequence of such acts ostensibly aimed at answering either a theoretical or practical question. Conversationalists often play symmetrical roles, while in other cases one speaker is doing a different conversational job from the others. For instance, in *didactic* conversations, one interlocutor aims to lead others to accept an answer to a practical or theoretical question about which the speaker may already have an opinion or plan, while in *Socratic* conversations, an interlocutor aims to lead others to answers by helping them to formulate their own views or plans of action. Soliloquys, in which we carry on conversations with ourselves, might be either of these kinds.

Some main types of conversation are displayed in Table 5.2. In symmetrical inquiries, speakers pool their information on the way to answering a question about how things are. In symmetrical deliberations we pool information and take into account our preferences as we work to formulate a plan of joint action. In didactic inquiries, one speaker answers a question for an audience; one familiar case of this is an academic lecture, while another is the telling of a story. A didactic deliberation is one in which a speaker tells others how to do something. In a Socratic deliberation, one speaker elicits from another a plan for getting something done. Six different types of conversation are displayed in Table 5.2.

---

4. Stalnaker, whose work in this area has been highly influential, defines common ground as follows: A proposition P is common ground between agents A and B just in case both A and B accept P, both accept that both accept P, both accept that both accept that both accept P, and so on (2014, p. 25). Stalnaker calls publicly observable events that become part of common ground manifest events. See Stalnaker 2014, p. 47 for further discussion.

TABLE 5.2. A Taxonomy of Conversation Types

	Inquiry	Deliberation
Symmetrical:	Speakers pool their information to answer a theoretical question.	Speakers pool their information and calibrate desires to answer a practical question.
Asymmetrical: didactic	One speaker answers a theoretical question for her audience.	One speaker shows or tells others how to do something, thereby answering a practical question for them.
Asymmetrical: Socratic	One speaker leads another to answer a theoretical question for herself.	One speaker leads another to answer a practical question for herself.

Our suggestion now is that illocutionary acts as first described by Austin, and then refined by Searle, may be placed within the larger structure of conversations. The partition into six types helps us to understand how illocutionary acts work in unison to aid speakers in achieving their goals.

5.4. Infelicities: Misfires and Abuses

In addition to his tripartition among locutionary, illocutionary, and perlocutionary acts, Austin also sheds light on the ways in which illocutionary acts may go wrong. On the one hand, certain speech acts are subject to *abuse*: the paradigm cases here are ones in which a speaker lies, for instance by making a statement she does not believe to be true, makes a promise she has no intention of following through on, or places a bet in a situation in which she has no way of paying up if she loses. Notice that in such cases, the putative speech act (promise, statement, or bet) does take place, but we are likely to feel that the speaker has exploited the institution supporting it in order to cut a corner. Observe as well that these norms governing speech acts bleed into ethical and legal territory: one who lies or makes a promise she knows she cannot keep will usually be felt to have done something not just conversationally inappropriate but also morally wrong, while placing a bet that one cannot cover will violate the law in some jurisdictions.

Abuses contrast starkly with what Austin calls *misfires*, which many students new to this topic find to be a subtle notion. As the image of a misfire suggests, a putative illocutionary act that misfires does not manage to be an act of the alleged kind at all. My attempt to name a building after myself, when it already has a name and I lack any legal authority to change its name, will be a locutionary act: I do manage to say the words "I hereby name this building Mitchell Green Hall." However, I have not thereby named anything; that is, I have not given the building a new moniker, even if I think that I have. (To speak with Kripke, discussed in Chapter 4: I have not succeeded in fixing the reference of the name 'Mitch Green Hall.') As a result, although I set out to perform an illocutionary act, I have failed. A similar failure can beset alleged promises in which it is mutually obvious to both speaker and hearer that the former could not possibly perform the act in question. Even alleged statements may misfire. This might be difficult to see because at least historically, philosophers have been in the habit of using 'sentence,' 'proposition,' 'statement,' and 'assertion' interchangeably. One who uses these terms interchangeably will tend to think that a locutionary act of uttering an indicative sentence must also be an assertion. Suppose, however, that it is CG between us that nothing is wrong with my clothing, and in particular that neither my pants nor anything else I am wearing is combusting. Suppose as well that I now utter the sentence

5.9. My pants are on fire.

Even though it is clear that I have said$_{thin}$ that my pants are on fire, it will be difficult for you to take me as having asserted this. More likely you will search around for an alternative interpretation, such as that I'm speaking hyperbolically (they're really just warm), or metaphorically (they're super-fashionable), or using a third figure of speech you've never heard of. In none of those cases, though, do I assert that my pants are combusting. Here, then, is a case of a locutionary act of uttering an indicative sentence that would seem to fail to be an assertion.

To follow Austin's slightly twee terminology, let us say that abuses and misfires constitute two kinds of *infelicity*. Part of the interest in the doctrine of infelicities is that it opens up the possibility of an illocutionary failure that is no fault of the speaker, but rather is due to injustice within her social milieu. (This will be a major topic for Chapter 7.)

A second source of interest in illocutionary misfires arises when we reflect back on Strawson's objection to Russell's account of definite descriptions. We noted that Strawson is widely taken to have argued against Russell that when a descriptive phrase is used in a situation in which the phrase's existence condition is not met, the sentence is neither true nor false (rather than merely false as Russell would have it).

However, we may now observe that this conclusion is not mandated by the data that Strawson presents in its favor. We might instead conclude that trying to assert that the present King of France is bald is a bit like trying to name an already-named building after myself: in both cases, I perform a locutionary act, but my attempted illocutionary act will fail. Accordingly, rather than follow Strawson in holding that presupposition failure begets truth-value gaps, another option is to suggest that such failure generates illocutionary misfires.

A third source of interest in infelicities lies in their ability to offer clues to the norms that we spend large parts of our lives conforming to without noticing. One can go a lifetime respecting norms of personal space (which dictate how far one is supposed to sit or stand from a person when speaking to her in person) without being aware of the size of that space or its tendency to vary from one society to another. So, too, we can chatter our lives away without attending to the complex norms that govern such behavior.

As we reflect on the types of infelicity that can affect speech acts, we might also wonder why various speech acts come with the normative structure that they do. Could there, for example, be assertions in which telling the truth did not even matter? Well, some speakers make assertions with no concern for the truth.[5] However, if all, or most, or even a preponderance of speakers started to make assertions with no concern for whether what they said is true, much of our practice of communication would begin to erode. If someone's making a statement is not even an indication that what he says is true, or at least that he believes what he says, we would eventually stop paying attention to what comes out of his mouth. We would all become boys who cry wolf, and after a while others' speech might start to sound—as Cratylus would put it—like banging on a brazen pot.

5.5. Indirect Speech Acts

We often get others to do things by making them aware of our or needs, wants, or interests, or by drawing attention to facts affecting theirs. Suppose A approaches her partner B while displaying a sealed jar of olives and says, "I can't seem to get this open." B will likely feel she is being

---

5. The phenomenon has even earned a technical term: "bullshit." See Frankfurt (2009) for fuller discussion.

asked to try to open the jar. Or at a concert in which we're all trying to get a view of the stage, I might say to the tall person standing in front of me, "You make a better door than a window." In so doing, I am indicating that the person is making it hard for me to see the stage, and a helpful response would be for the addressee to make room to permit me a better view. My remark is a polite, or at least roundabout, way of doing what I might more bluntly have done with a simple, "Please move." Similarly, "You missed a spot," said to someone cleaning a window is naturally heard as a suggestion that the addressee go back and clean the area he missed.

One may easily be impressed by the ingenuity with which speakers get their needs met while being comparatively polite. Consider some expressions commonly used to assist in this purpose:

5.10. *Would you mind if* I borrowed your pen for a moment?
5.11. *Do you think you might be able to* lend me 10 euros?
5.12. *Could I trouble you for* a sheet of paper?

We readily imagine 5.10 being used to get the addressee to lend the speaker her pen, 5.11 being used to ask to borrow 10 euros, and 5.12 being used to ask to borrow a sheet of paper. One approach to these phenomena might be to hypothesize that sentences such as these are ambiguous: perhaps in some contexts, the speaker of 5.11 is really saying

5.13. Please lend me 10 euros.

Perhaps, but the suggestion raises many questions in turn. For one, we know from Chapter 1 that the only way for a sentence to be ambiguous is by virtue either of lexical ambiguity or structural ambiguity. In the former case, we would need to know which word or words take on an atypical meaning here. (Where, for instance, would you propose to find lexical ambiguity in 5.11, and how would you use such posited ambiguity to arrive at 5.13?) In the latter case, we would need to know how any of the sentences in question take on different logical forms while their words retain their usual meanings, and how any of those logical forms is naturally seen as helping to effect the putative speech act.

Might there be a more plausible route for explaining these data? As Searle (1979b) emphasizes, a roundabout way of indicating what you'd like someone to do is to ask about or otherwise draw her attention to the conditions that need to be met for her to do that thing. These conditions might include your physical limitations (such as whether you're tall enough to reach a certain shelf), your preferences (such as whether you would mind moving a bit to the left), or your moral or legal constraints (such as whether you're allowed to let me see that document). By drawing your attention to any of these constraints, I might also give you reason to think that I'd like you to do something that depends on one or more of those constraints being met. This is why questions such as

5.14. Are you able to reach the blue jar on that shelf?
5.15. Have you seen my black coat?
5.16. Are you allowed to let me see that document?

are, respectively, often understood as requests to grab the blue jar, to help find a coat, or to show me a document. Observe, though, that being *understood* as a request does not make an utterance into a request. This is why we do well to be on our guard around discussions of what are known as *indirect speech acts*. Theorists of speech acts like to draw our attention to cases such as

5.17. Can you pass the salt?

When uttered by one diner to another, this is normally, perhaps even conventionally, understood as an indirect request that the addressee pass the salt. "Indirect" here means that an utterance of 5.17 serves in some way to perform an illocution different from, or in addition to, the one suggested by its grammatical form. Grammatically, one might expect 5.17 to be used in the asking of a question, but in the scenario we have imagined, it is also, or is instead, being used to make a request. The last sentence contained a hedge because different options present themselves for describing what is going on in these cases. On one option, we might suppose that the speaker of 5.17 is performing two illocutions, one of which is a question and the other a request. On the other, the speaker is only seeming to pose a question, but is in fact just making a request. The latter hypothesis might seem more economical and thus preferable. On the two–speech act approach, we would want an explanation of how addressees manage to figure out which speech act is the one that's more appropriate to respond to. Perhaps they are able to discern that one speech act is in some sense more primary than the other. By contrast, on the "one–speech act" approach, we would need to account for how the reply, "Yes, I can," followed by no salt passing, would seem to be a legitimate if smart-alecky response.

We might also wonder whether the act that is alleged to be performed indirectly (the request to hold the door open, pass the salt, show me the document, etc.) must be construed as a speech act at all. If A sees B reach for something that she cannot quite get to, A can reasonably conclude that B is trying to get that thing. Simply reaching for something is not a way of requesting it. On the other hand, so acting tends to manifest one's desire for the thing being sought. (After all, one good way of finding out what a person wants is to see what he's trying to get.) Further, we sometimes reach for a thing with the aim of letting others know what we want. Recalling our account of expression from Chapter 2, we know that when we not only manifest our state of mind, but do so with the intention of making that state known, or at least knowable to others, then we also *express* that state of mind. Perhaps in this light we may consider certain so-called indirect speech acts as expressions rather than illocutions?[6]

Our suggestion is then that while nothing prevents a speaker from having the complex set of intentions requisite to perform a speech indirectly, many cases often construed as indirect speech acts are more parsimoniously construed as ways of expressing psychological states to which others may be expected to respond appropriately. If I express a want for something that you have or are able to get, that gives you some reason to provide me with it; if I express fear of something else that you can keep from harming me or someone I care about, that gives you a reason to help out, and so on. Following our precept that the more parsimonious theory is preferable to the less parsimonious unless we have good independent reasons for preferring the latter, we may tentatively accept that for many cases often construed as indirect speech acts, we do better to construe them as expressive rather than illocutionary acts.

It would seem, then, that we have a range of options for understanding indirect speech acts: perhaps they involve two speech acts (one direct, the other indirect), or instead just one (performed indirectly), or perhaps they just enable the speaker to express a state of mind to which her addressee may be expected to provide an appropriate response. It may instead be that no one of these three accounts quite works for the range of cases that may interest us, and different types of case call for different treatment.

---

6. Without using the notion of expression, Bertolet (1994) raises doubts as to whether all alleged indirect speech acts need to be seen as illocutionary acts.

5.6. Study Questions and Suggestions for Further Reading

Study Questions

1. Bearing in mind example 5.8 ("You'll be more punctual in the future"), please construct your own case in which a speaker makes an utterance in which it is clear what she has said, but not clear how she means it.

2. After considering Strawson's critique of Austin's view that all speech acts depend on extra-semantic conventions, please try to find examples of other speech acts (besides those that Strawson mentions) that do not conform to Austin's conventionalist model.

3. Would you expect to encounter variation in what speech acts are performed from one culture to another, either at a time, or over time? Please explain your answer. Also, if you would expect to encounter such variation, what might account for that variation?

4. Please construct your own example of an indirect speech act, or at least one that Searle would treat as such. Might such a case also be understood in more parsimonious terms as an act of expression? Please explain your answer.

5. Is it possible to perform an illocutionary act without using words, say with a (wordless) emoji or a gif? Please explain your answer, and if you answer in the affirmative, consider the objection that such acts are expressive rather than illocutionary.

Further Reading (with recommended [*] items for instructors)

The classic historical text for speech act theory is Austin (1962),* followed closely by Searle (1969).* Sbisà (2007) provides useful exegetical insights on Austin's text. Anscombe (1957) is a probing investigation of the notion of intention and is the source of the idea of direction of fit. Strawson (1964)* famously challenges Austin's conventionalism about illocutionary force, advocating speaker intentions as an alternative concept for understanding the force of speech acts that are not essentially conventional. Strawson is here building on Grice's* (1957) crucial notion of speaker meaning. Kemmerling (2013) provides a careful discussion of various accounts of speaker meaning put forward subsequent to Grice's original formulation. Stalnaker (2014) articulates his notion of common ground and its significance for pragmatic theorizing. Green (2017) advocates ways of extending Stalnaker's approach to cases such as fictional discourse. Searle (1979b)* is the canonical work for the theory of indirect speech acts. Bertolet challenges Searle's analysis. Green (2020) offers an overview of speech act theory. Fogal, Harris, and Moss (2018) is a collection of recent papers on speech act theory, and it includes an insightful introductory essay by the editors. Frankfurt (2009) is the go-to discussion of bullshit.

References

Anscombe, G. 1957. *Intention.* Malden, MA: Blackwell.

Austin, J. L. 1962. *How to Do Things with Words.* 2nd ed. Edited by J. O. Urmson and Sbisa. Cambridge, MA: Harvard University Press.

Bertolet, R. 1994. "Are There Indirect Speech Acts?" In *Foundations of Speech Act Theory: Philosophical and Linguistic Perspectives*, edited by S. Tsohatizis, 335–349. London: Routledge.

Fogal, D., Harris, D., and Moss, M. 2018. *New Work on Speech Acts.* Oxford: Oxford University Press.

Frankfurt, H. 2009. *On Bullshit.* Princeton, NJ: Princeton University Press.

Green, M. 2017. "Conversation and Common Ground." *Philosophical Studies* 174: 1587–1604.

Green, M. 2020. "Speech Acts." In *Stanford Encyclopedia of Philosophy*, edited by Edward Zalta. https://plato.stanford.edu/

Grice, P. 1957. "Meaning." In *Studies in the Way of Words*, 213–223. Cambridge, MA: Harvard University Press.

Kemmerling, A. 2013. "Speaker's Meaning." In *Pragmatics of Speech Actions*, edited by M. Sbisà and K. Turner, 77–106. Berlin: de Gruyter.

Sbisà, M. 2007. "How to Read Austin." *Pragmatics* 17: 461–473.

Searle, J. 1969. *Speech Acts: An Essay in the Philosophy of Language.* Cambridge: Cambridge University Press.

Searle, J. 1979a. "A Taxonomy of Illocutionary Acts." Reprinted in *Expression and Meaning: Studies in the Theory of Speech Acts*, 1–29. Cambridge: Cambridge University Press.

Searle, J. 1979b. "Indirect Speech Acts." Reprinted in *Expression and Meaning: Studies in the Theory of Speech Acts*, 30–56. Cambridge: Cambridge University Press.

Searle, J., and Vanderveken, D. 1985. *Foundations of Illocutionary Logic.* Cambridge: Cambridge University Press.

Stalnaker, R. 2014. *Context.* Oxford: Oxford University Press.

Strawson, P. 1950. "On Referring." *Mind* 59: 320–344.

Strawson, P. 1952. *Introduction to Logical Theory.* London: Methuen.

Strawson, P. 1964. "Intention and Convention in Speech Acts." *Philosophical Review* 73: 439–460.

Williamson, T. 1996. "Knowing and Asserting." *Philosophical Review* 105: 489–523.

CHAPTER 6

Context Sensitivity, Implicature, and Presupposition

Chapter Overview

We begin with a well-studied form of context sensitivity known as indexicality, in which the semantic content of an expression depends on the context in which it is used; we will also relate indexicality to the intension/extension distinction developed in Chapter 4. From there we turn to the notion of implicature, in which a speaker means more than she says, and in ways that often rely on implicitly understood conversational norms. We then return to the notion of presupposition and explore some reasons for construing it as a pragmatic rather than a semantic phenomenon. The chapter ends with a look at explicature, in which pragmatic factors help to determine what is said in ways that go beyond indexicality.

6.1. Indexicals: Character and Content

Some expressions are so designed that their content depends in a systematic way on the context in which they are uttered; these are known as indexicals. That might seem like a simple idea, but it is a powerful one. Recall that in Chapter 4 we introduced the concept of extension as a tool for correlating expressions (such as nouns, verbs, or sentences) with sets (whose members might be individual objects, ordered n-tuples of objects, or truth values). We then noted that a term's extension might vary from one situation to another, and that point motivated introduction of the concept of intension, which is a function from such situations, or possible worlds, to extensions. We will now introduce the concept of *character*, which is a function from contexts of utterance to intensions, and widely thought of as a more accurate tool for characterizing linguistic meaning than is intension.

We noted before that 'I' has a meaning that is independent of anyone's using it on a particular occasion; yet it is also clear that if we see or hear a tokening of 'I am hungry' there is an important sense in which we do not know what has been said until we find out who uttered that sentence. Furthermore, there are strong grounds for holding that once that word is tokened, it refers rigidly to the speaker, rather than flexibly, to, say, whoever may utter it in some counterfactual situation. Think of the character of 'I,' then, as being a function whose input is the information that a particular speaker has uttered that word, and whose output is an intension, that is a function from worlds to extensions. It is a further claim that this intension is constant in the sense of being a rigid designator. Is that claim true? Evidence for it emerges as we observe that an utterance such as the following may well be true:

6.1. I might not have been speaking.

Suppose that 6.1 is uttered by Eusebia. In that case, Eusebia is speaking, but she notes rightly that this fact is not a necessary truth about her: someone else might have cut her off before she got a word out, or made it to the podium before she did. In that situation, the word 'I' as uttered in 6.1 would not refer to that usurper, but to Eusebia. Further reflection on similar examples concerning counterfactual situations, will, I suspect, convince you that once 'I' has been uttered felicitously, it will track its utterer across counterfactual situations in a manner similar to a rigidly designating proper name.

Other words in English with similar properties include 'here' (which rigidly designates the location of the context in which it is uttered), 'you' (rigidly designating the addressee of the context of utterance), and 'now' (rigidly designating the time of the context of utterance). But what is a *context of utterance*? This is another technical notion that refers to parameters of a situation in which a linguistic item is, or could be, uttered. It is usually defined as having a unique speaker, as well as a unique location, time, one or more addressees, and possible world at which it occurs. We might also include in the context of utterance a domain of discourse (in the sense of that expression used in Chapter 3), providing a set of objects over which quantifiers range. For purposes of modeling the behavior of words like 'this' and 'that,' often accompanied by a physical act of pointing, it might also include a ranking of objects in terms of their degree of perceptual or cognitive salience. Similarly, for purposes of interpreting vague expressions such as 'bald,' 'red,' or 'hexagonal,' context of utterance might also include a standard of precision. Even with all this apparatus, the concept of a context of utterance is a large idealization, since actual contexts of utterance might have multiple speakers (such as when people jointly take a vow), no addressee (such as when we think out loud), and a location whose boundaries are indeterminate (since 'here' can refer to a minute area under intense magnification, and at other times to our planet or even galaxy). In practice, however, a theorist will specify a notion of utterance context that will suit her purposes, which themselves are generally set by the area of discourse she wishes to investigate.

We may now define *indexicals* as words or expressions whose content varies systematically with features of the context of utterance. On this approach, all words and expressions have a character, but indexicals have characters that yield different intensions at different contexts of utterance. The numeral '8' refers, let us suppose, to the number 8, but its content is the same no matter who utters it. It is therefore not an indexical. Also, we should not confuse indexicality with lexical ambiguity. Strictly, there is nothing lexically ambiguous about 'I,' 'here,' or 'now,' since their linguistic meaning does not vary from one speaker or speaking to another. That is different from, say, the way in which 'bat' might be the name of a winged mammal or of an artifact used in the game of baseball.

Philosophers of language often distinguish "pure" indexicals from others that are "impure." The pure ones (such as those already mentioned) acquire intensions in ways that are relatively free from speaker intentions and accompanying gestures. On the other hand, *demonstratives* are special types of indexicals that in their most basic uses depend on accompanying gestures for their interpretation. At least in its most basic use, 'this' is accompanied by a manual gesture of pointing to an object that is in the foreground of a perceptual field, usually but not exclusively the visual field. ('That' in its demonstrative use is similar, but it may also refer to entities that are not in the perceptual foreground.) Theorists have debated the question whether the reference of one of these words gets secured by the speaker's intentions, or instead by the geometrical features of their pointing gestures, such as by a line determined by a pointing finger; or by some combination of these factors.[1] Also, brief reflection will reveal that we also use 'this' and 'that' to refer to items outside of perceptual consciousness, but that still have cognitive salience.

Just how pervasive is indexicality? While 'I', 'here', 'now' and the like are uncontroversial examples, and many would supplement the list with demonstratives such as 'this' and 'that', so-called *contextualists* have argued that other expressions in ordinary language have intensions that are in subtle ways dependent on the context in which they are uttered. An example of such a view is *epistemic contextualism*, according to which 'know' and its cognates depend in subtle ways for their intensions on the context in which they are uttered, and more precisely upon the epistemic standards that are prevalent in that context of utterance. Thus when we use 'know' in an everyday, un-self-conscious way, we have no difficulty claiming that, say, we know that the sun will rise tomorrow, and fully expect that others will not demur. Here the intension of 'know' is one that requires justification for our beliefs, but not also absolute certainty that those beliefs are correct. On the other hand, a skeptic intervening in the conversation might ask, "But do you *know* that it will rise tomorrow? After all it's *possible* that overnight our planet will be hit by a fast-moving asteroid as happens in the movie *Melancholia*." If interlocutors respond by taking the challenge seriously, they will implicitly have allowed the intension of 'know' to shift to include a requirement of absolute certainty. Further, this shift may occur without interlocutors being aware that it has.[2]

Another reason for interest in indexicality is its connection with a priori knowledge. Imagine that you've just undergone major surgery that required general anesthesia. You're now regaining consciousness as the drug wears off, and wake up in a dark and silent room. For a brief moment you may be at a loss to know where you are or what just happened. In a Cartesian spirit, you decide to build up from solid foundations. One such foundation you can be sure of is expressed by:

6.2. I am here now.

---

1. For further discussion see for instance Kaplan (1989) and Reimer (1991).
2. Lewis 1979 provides a vivid account of how the skeptic can subtly change the intension of 'know.'

This seems like something that you can know before you settle other questions, and more precisely without having to settle any empirical questions. If that is correct, then that sentence expresses a thought that you can know a priori to be true. On the other hand, the thought thus expressed is contingent: you might not have been there at that place and time in the hospital, but instead could have been discharged early or have perished under the knife. If these considerations are correct, we may conclude that the thought expressed by 'I am here now' is both contingent and a priori.[3]

Indexicality, both as it applies to pure indexicals and to impure cases such as demonstratives, is widely regarded as a paradigm case of *saturation*.[4] The thought behind this term is that pragmatic factors that are determined by features of the context of utterance are invoked in settling, for instance, what time 'now' refers to, who 'y'all' picks out, the set of items over which quantifiers range, and, possibly, what standards have to be met for an individual to know that P. Further, assuming that any ambiguities have been resolved, the saturation process is now complete and we now have a content, which for current purposes is represented as an intension. The crucial thought is that the saturation process needs to do its work before a word, phrase, or sentence may be said to express an intension. As we will see later (Section 6.4), some authors have argued that pragmatic factors needed for saturation are more pervasive and far-reaching than even this picture suggests.

6.2. Implicature: Conventional, Conversational, and Beyond

Misuses of language take many forms, some of which violate rules of etiquette such as occurs when we address someone by the wrong title or mispronounce their name. Other misuses involve violation of norms that we might suggest to be distinctively conversational. Consider this brief exchange from the Monty Python movie *Life of Brian*. A Centurion enters a dungeon-like staging area where prisoners are waiting to

---

3. Garcia-Carpintero (2008) discusses contingent a priori truths in greater detail.

4. Some authors use the phrase 'the pragmatic determination of what is said,' but given the controversial nature of the notion of 'what is said,' we prefer the less freighted term 'saturation.'

be crucified. He is looking for Brian and whoever else might be accompanying him, and demands of two attendants:

> Centurion: Are they gone!?
> Attendant: We've got lumps of it round the back!

The attendant's response is quite irrelevant to the Centurion's question, and naturally leaves the latter perplexed. More generally, when we speak to one another, we expect our conversational contributions to be relevant to whatever might be at issue, whether it be the whereabouts of people slated to be crucified, or something more mundane such as what time the next bus comes or whether we need more eggs for the dish we're planning. Indeed, the norm of relevance is so deeply ingrained in our everyday practice that it is difficult purposefully to say something wholly irrelevant to another's remark, and furthermore to have him understand it *as* irrelevant rather than search for some way of construing it that would be relevant. (Try it.)

Further, even when what we say is perfectly clear, our interlocutors may find themselves puzzled over a possible further message we have in mind in saying what we do. Sometimes, of course, we do not mean what we say, such as in cases of irony: you remark, "Nice job!" as the vase slips out of my hands, shattering on the floor. (Presumably you didn't mean that my blunder was a nice job.) In other cases we mean what we say but something more as well, and in either case the meaning that is distinct from our words might be due to conventions associated with those words, while in other cases it is not. These two categories correspond to Grice's distinction between conventional and nonconventional implicature.

Conventional implicature: Some words seem conventionally designed to enable us to mean more than we say. Grice (1989) would suggest, for instance, that the following two sentences have the same truth conditions, yet differ in one important respect:

6.3.   Gregor was brown-eyed and intelligent.
6.4.   Gregor was brown-eyed but intelligent.

Unlike 6.3, someone who illocutes 6.4 would generate confusion among her listeners. Why think that eye color would make someone less likely to be intelligent than otherwise? The choice of "but" rather than "and" seems to commit the speaker to there being some conflict or tension between having a certain eye color and intelligence. To see why, imagine someone uttering the second of these but with an attempt to walk back the unspoken implication:

6.5. Gregor was brown-eyed but intelligent, which is not for a moment to suggest a conflict or tension between eye color and intelligence.

Such a remark will likely provoke a response such as "Then why did you say 'but'?!" Nonetheless, Grice also contends that 6.3 and 6.4 have the same truth conditions, namely those given by the conjunction of 'Gregor was brown-eyed' and 'Gregor was intelligent.' Grice's idea is that an aspect of the meaning of 'but' goes beyond 'and' to suggest a contrast or conflict between properties expressed by the two sentences flanking it. The contrast, however, is not part of what the speaker says$_{thick}$ but is instead implied by her choice of that word.

A conventionally implicating word, then, conveys what it does by virtue of its meaning, but what it conveys is only implied rather than communicated explicitly: it is not part of what the speaker says$_{thick}$ and does not contribute to the truth conditions of her utterance.[5] We will return to the notion of conventional implicature when we discuss slurs in the next chapter.

Grice famously distinguished between conventional and nonconventional implicature. Students of his work sometimes fail to notice that the latter category is the broader class of which conversational implicature is a member. Box 6.1 helps explain Grice's way of thinking about

---

5. Bach (1999) challenges Grice's way of understanding conventional implicature by arguing that the alleged conventionally implicating words contribute to what speakers say. In support of his argument he offers what he calls the

IQ Test: An element of a sentence contributes to what is said in an utterance of that sentence if and only if there can be an accurate and complete indirect quotation of the utterance (in the same language) that includes that element, or a corresponding element, in the "that" clause that specifies what is said. (1999, p. 340)

Bach proceeds to apply the IQ Test to sentences containing words like "but," and finds that accurate and complete indirect quotations do include that word. However, it is not clear what this shows. Even if it is true that an accurate and complete indirect quotation of 6.4 is 'Nahid said that Gregor is brown-eyed but intelligent,' all this establishes is that 'but' contributes to what a speaker says. That, however, would not challenge anything that Grice claims. Instead, it would only challenge Grice's position if it could also be shown that 'but' contributes something different to what is said than does 'and.' This is precisely the question at issue, and it is not settled by Bach's IQ test or other considerations that he adduces.

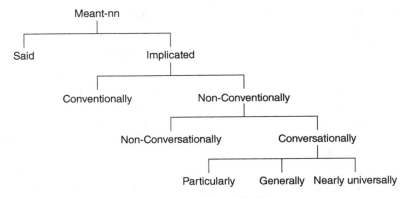

FIGURE 6.1 Forms of speaker-meaning (meaning-nn) in Grice

the different forms that speaker-meaning (he used the term "meaning-nn") may take. Observe that while nothing can be both said and implicated, in a single speech act, a speaker might say one thing and implicate another.

What might be a case of implicature that is neither conventional nor conversational? This would have to be a case of speaker-meaning something that does not depend wholly on linguistic conventions but also does not depend on conversational norms. We will return later to offer a suggestion as to what might fill this category.

Conversational implicature: More far-reaching than Grice's notion of conventional implicature was his theory, or proto-theory, of conversational implicature (Grice 1989). He proposed that many of our verbal exchanges are governed by a background set of norms that we might spend our lives following without knowing that we are doing so. Further, if we do take notice of such norms, we begin to see that a speech act may have a true content while still violating a conversational norm. The attendant who says, "We've got lumps of it round the back!" may well be speaking truly in spite of failing to answer the Centurion's question. So, too, if I remark that you are not identical to the Peloponnesian War, what I say is quite true (I hope!) while being irrelevant to nearly all conceivable conversations in which we might be participating.

Furthermore, supposing our verbal exchanges are often carried out against the background of a set of norms, we would expect interlocutors to presume each other to be adhering to those norms. For this reason, apparent violations of such norms tend to lead others to suspect that we might mean more than we have said. Suppose a student of mine has never shown evidence of intoxication in class. She now raises her hand, and before allowing her to speak, I remark:

Justine, I'm glad to see that you're sober today.

Justine and her classmates might be perplexed by what I say, and naturally take me to be suggesting that she has a tendency to be inebriated in class. Were someone to press me on the point, I might reply that I was just stating a fact, to which someone might rejoin:

What you say is true, but it's misleading.

How could saying something perfectly true be misleading? It is misleading, one might offer, to make such a remark because doing so suggests that it could be useful to settling a question that was on any of our minds (such as "Is Justine sober today?"), when in fact no such question is on our minds.

These phenomena of an utterance being true but misleading, and the related one of speakers meaning more than they say, offer a limitation on what the Ordinary Language philosopher (OLP) can establish with her methods. The reason is that the OLP offers a critique of traditional philosophical problems as depending on misuses of language. In response, this new approach points out that not all misuses are created equal: some might involve category mistakes, others might violate grammatical rules, but for all the OLP has shown, the ones that concern her might just involve violation of conversational norms. In the latter case, the suspect utterances (such as "Dmitri scratched his earlobe of his own free will") might still be true, if misleading, and still enable formulation of the traditional problems.

Not only does this response to OLP limit its ability to dissolve traditional philosophical questions, it also points the way to an explanation of how speakers mean more than they say, or, in other cases something different from what they say. That style of explanation is integral to the concept of *conversational implicature*. This is a term of art introduced by Grice for the purpose of capturing a type of nonconventional meaning whose generation depends on interaction between our utterance, our intentions, and a shared background of conversational norms. For illustration, consider the following four sentences:

6.6. Juanita took the medicine and got better.
6.7. Juanita took the medicine.

6.8. Juanita's taking the medicine preceded her getting better.

6.9. Juanita's taking the medicine is causally responsible for her getting better.

6.6 logically entails 6.7. However, while a speaker who utters 6.6 will normally be understood as suggesting 6.8, this latter implication is not an entailment of 6.6. We can confirm this by noting that a speaker of 6.6 can go on to deny 6.8 without contradicting herself, as in:

6.10. Juanita took the medicine and got better, though not necessarily in that order.

What, then, enables us to hear 6.8 as being in some sense implied by the utterance of 6.6? Grice's answer is that speakers typically, if unconsciously, adhere to a nonrigid norm, which he calls the Maxim of Manner, enjoining them to narrate events in the order in which they took place. This norm is nonrigid because we sometimes narrate events in order of importance rather than in temporal order, and at other times merely as they occur to us. However, on the assumption of a default in narrative structure corresponding to that of temporal order, we can make sense of one way in which speakers convey more than they say.

Implicature is pervasive in many cultures and among those who know one another moderately well. Chapter 1 led off with an example of a friend asking, "How's that working out for you?," which may be seen as another case of this phenomenon: the speaker posed a question, but she may well also have been suggesting that the pursuit that she was asking about was ill-conceived. The phenomenon of "damning with faint praise" points to another case of implicature: a tepid compliment often conveys a veiled criticism, as in "These were some of the roundest hamburgers I've ever eaten!" After all, if that's the most that can be said for the burgers, it's not likely that the speaker found them particularly tasty.

Grice hypothesized that conversations are carried out against a background of norms that divide into two parts: one is an overarching Principle, and the others are maxims that may be seen as constraints on its application[6]:

A natural first reaction on encountering the Cooperative Principle (CP) is to suspect it of vacuity, as it seems to enjoin speakers to say what

---

6. See Grice 1989, pp. 28–29. Note that Grice appears to use 'talk exchange' and 'conversation' interchangeably, but we have been using the former in a more liberal, and the latter in a more demanding sense.

the conversation requires them to say. However, CP makes reference to the accepted purpose or direction of one's talk-exchange, or conversation, suggesting the substantial claim that these activities have such a purpose or direction. This is not, of course, to suggest that there is one purpose or direction that all conversations have, but rather that all such conversations have some purpose or other.

BOX 6.1   GRICE'S COOPERATIVE PRINCIPLE AND SUPPORTING CONVERSATIONAL MAXIMS

Cooperative Principle: Make your contribution one that is required, at the stage at which it occurs, by the accepted purpose or direction of the talk-exchange in which you are engaged.

Maxim of Quality

Supermaxim:

Try to make your contribution one that is true.

Submaxims:

Do not say what you believe to be false.
Do not say that for which you lack adequate evidence.

Maxim of Quantity

Make your contribution as informative as is required (for the current purposes of the exchange).
Do not make your contribution more informative than is required.

Maxim of Relevance

Be relevant.

Maxim of Manner

Supermaxim:

Be perspicuous.

Submaxims:

Avoid obscurity of expression.
Avoid ambiguity.
Be brief (avoid unnecessary prolixity).
Be orderly.

In fact, in Chapter 5 we have already considered a variety of conversation types in which interlocutors might engage, and each of these types builds in a purpose, namely to answer a theoretical or practical question. Accordingly, if for instance you know that you are engaging in an asymmetrical didactic inquiry, this will impose particular constraints on what you should say, which constraints will be different from those that flow from being in another of the six general types of conversation that we identified in Table 5.2.

Knowing how to be cooperative in making a particular utterance demands awareness of the type of conversation in which we are engaged, as well as the particular aim that is guiding it, such as what question we are trying to answer. It also requires knowing how much progress we have made in answering that question. (Failure to heed the latter condition tends to make us repetitive.)

A conversational implicature may be generated by following the CP and related maxims, such as we saw in the Juanita cases earlier. However, an implicature may also be generated by one's violation of one or more of the maxims. We are often, for instance, willfully irrelevant, ostentatiously verbose, and insufficiently informative. In so doing, we also often lead those who receive our messages to ponder why we are violating conversational norms. One hypothesis that might be entertained is that the speaker means more, or something other, than what she says. So long as the speaker intends to be so understood, that is good reason to think that she has conversationally implicated a content beyond what she says.

Like conventional implicatures, Grice sees conversational implicatures as being cases of speaker meaning. One cannot therefore conversationally imply something inadvertently, and just because someone takes one to be doing so, even justifiably, does not show her to be correct. Similarly, although we will qualify the point later, it is speakers and not sentences who conversationally imply things.

Different implicatures may be understood relative to the four maxim types of Quantity, Quality, Relation, and Manner. We have already seen one manner implicature in action, although it did not involve violation of that norm. For such a case, imagine someone is wordy in the course of what could have been a banal request:

Would you be so kind as to remove your feet from my desk?

The speaker could just have said, "Please take your feet off my desk," and her not doing so raises the question why. One hypothesis is that the speaker is implying that her addressee is so obtuse about matters of etiquette that he needs special handling in order to get him to do something that any properly behaved person would do as a matter of course.

For a case of quantity implicature, imagine someone who knows more than she lets on and answers a question that is guiding conversation in a way that is clearly less informative than she may have been expected to be. A teacher is passing back graded examination booklets to her students, one of whom asks, "How did we do on the exam?" She replies,

Some of the students passed the exam.

It is natural to construe her as indicating that not all students passed. For her diffidence is not due to her not knowing how many passed; after all, she just graded all the exams. Instead, she is most likely indicating some students did not pass. That is why her answer is likely to send a shudder through her classroom.

The *Life of Brian* example was not a case of relevance implicature, because there is no reason to think that the attendant was being irrelevant for the sake of getting across a point beyond what he said. (As emerges later in the scene, the attendant was probably just trying to distract the Centurion.) Instead, a speaker might be overtly irrelevant for the sake of communicating that the current course of conversation is potentially embarrassing or otherwise unwanted:

6.11. Word is that you lost a big sum at the casino last night.
6.12. Hey, did you hear the Alpaca Lips are playing this Friday at the County Fair?

The speaker of 6.12 might say what she does for the purpose of avoiding an embarrassing topic, but she might in saying what she does also speaker-mean that the conversation should address a different topic.

The most common way of violating the Quality maxim is by lying. However, if lying were to become too pervasive in a linguistic community, communication within that group would run the risk of breaking down since speakers would no longer be able to take what others say as having even prima facie likelihood of being true. In other cases, we violate Quality with the expectation that our addressees will notice that we are doing so, and for this reason cast around for another way of understanding our utterance. Cases such as hyperbole and irony are of this kind. We will return to irony in Chapter 7, but for a case of hyperbole, consider:

> The line to get into the show was a mile long, so we went for drinks instead.

The line in question might, of course, have been a mile long. However, more likely the speaker was exaggerating the length of the line. Why would she do so? One suggestion is that she meant to imply that the line was too long to be worth waiting on, while also providing her addressee with a visual image that would help him understand why the task of getting into the club seemed overwhelming.

Grice distinguishes between what he calls particularized and generalized conversational implicature. These two notions mark ends of a spectrum, but what matters for our purposes is that the former are highly dependent on parameters of context for their generation, while the latter are less dependent in this way. Consider the following exchange:

> 6.13. How was work today?
> 6.14. Well, I lost a contact lens.

We automatically infer that the respondent lost one of her own contact lenses. However, if we subsequently learn that she works in a contact lens factory, we might refrain from drawing that conclusion. Accordingly, while it is tempting to see the respondent as having uttered a sentence whose literal meaning is that she has lost one of her own contact lenses, that conclusion could only be drawn from an unduly narrow body of data. It may nevertheless be harmless for a theorist to see the sentence 'I lost a contact lens' as conversationally implicating that the lens belonged to the speaker, so long as it is borne in mind that this way of speaking is a convenient shortcut for a more accurate way of describing matters in which speakers' intentions and the conversational context may always play a role.

Table 6.1 summarizes the main features of conventional and conversational implicature. We have already explained that both types of implicature are species of speaker meaning. Only the latter are cancelable, either implicitly, as occurs when we learn that the speaker of 6.14 works in a contact lens factory, or explicitly, as would occur if that speaker had offered the following in response to 6.13 rather than 6.14:

> 6.14. Well, I lost a contact lens, though fortunately not one of my own.

TABLE 6.1 Benchmarks for Conventional and Conversational Implicature

	Conventional implicature	Conversational implicature
Speaker-meant?	Yes	Yes
Cancelable?	No	Yes
Detachable?	Yes	No
Calculable?	No	Yes
Indeterminate?	No	Yes

An implicature is detachable if it is preserved even when the speaker says the same thing in a different way. It is calculable if the addressee or other observer of the utterance is able to construct a line of reasoning that would yield the conclusion that the speaker has implicated what she has. Finally, an implicature is indeterminate if, for any one attribution of what has been implicated, another attribution could be provided that would equally make sense of the speaker's utterance.

Nonconventional, nonconversational implicature: Box 6.1 leaves open the possibility of implicatures that are neither conventional nor conversational. Might any phenomena occupy that spot? Consider an overt scowl, that is, a facial expression of anger that is made intentionally but with the further intention of making that first intention manifest. As such, the scowling agent might mean that she is angry. She is not saying that she is angry, although she does seem to be implying it. Further, her behavior is governed neither by conventions (since scowling and like facial expressions are not convention-bound) nor by conversational maxims (since those maxims regulate illocutions only). It follows that the scowl made in such conditions falls into this rarely discussed category of implicature that is neither conventional nor conversational. The same point would seem to apply to other overtly made facial expressions, as well as certain gestures and uses of intonation.

6.3. Presupposition: Semantic and Pragmatic

We earlier encountered the concept of presupposition in discussion of Strawson's critique of Russell's theory of descriptions. Strawson argued that if a definite description involving a sentence like 'The current Queen of Iceland is rich' is uttered in a situation in which Iceland is not a monarchy, we would be disinclined to say that the sentence is false (as might seem to be predicted by Russell's account), but instead suggest that the question of the sentence's truth does not arise. Strawson and those who followed him moved from that observation to the conclusion that the sentence is neither true nor false, but in Chapter 5 we raised doubts whether that inference was mandated; another option might be that an attempt to use the sentence in an illocution is apt to misfire.

Nonetheless, for the quarter-century after Strawson's challenge to Russell, a large body of research flying under the "truth value gap" banner was produced in both logic and linguistics. In addition to definite descriptions, we also find presupposition-triggering expressions such as the following:

Factives: Jan regrets that he ate the cookies. (presupposes that Jan ate the cookies)

Cleft sentences: It was Jan who ate all the cookies. (presupposes that someone did.)

Too: Jan sneezed too. (presupposes that other people than Jan sneezed, or that Jan did something else besides sneezing)

Implicative verbs: Jan forgot to take his keys. (presupposes that Jan intended to take them)

Like description sentences, the four types exhibit the phenomenon that the putative presupposition is carried even when the sentence is negated. ('It wasn't Jan who ate all the cookies,' etc.) In the three decades following Strawson's critique, intensive investigation proceeded in search of a solution to the so-called *projection problem*: in addition to negation, what other embedding contexts enable the target presupposition to be a commitment of the speaker? Researchers distinguished between plugs (which prevented presupposition from rising to the top), holes (which did not prevent this), and filters (which let commitments through for some words but not for others).[7] However, as the machinery became more complex, the explanatory power of the enterprise dwindled. It begins to seem that we are engaged in the task of describing what various expressions do under different types of embedded context, rather than explaining that behavior. Furthermore, as Stalnaker (1975) argued, our intuitions about whether a presupposition

---

7. Soames (1989) provides a detailed account of this history.

failure should make for a truth-value gap, or instead a false but conversationally inappropriate utterance, are not robust. The result was that by approximately 1980, the semantic notion of presupposition was giving way to the pragmatic one.

According to this latter, pragmatic approach to presupposition, at the most basic level it is speakers who presuppose things. For a speaker to presuppose a content S is for her to take it for granted in her reasoning and behavior. Furthermore, according to the pragmatic approach to presupposition, insofar as there is a useful notion of what an expression presupposes, that notion should be explained in terms of what it is proper for a speaker to do with it. As a first approximation, a speaker should only utter an expression that tends to presuppose S if she takes S to be part of common ground, or if S can be added to CG without too much of an epistemic imposition on her addressees. The latter qualification is needed to account for so-called *informative presuppositions*, in which a speaker's utterance presupposes a content that was not previously in CG, but that interlocutors are willing to add to CG without argument. That plausibly occurs in such a case as:

I'm sorry I'm late, but my car had trouble starting.

Other people at the meeting might not have been aware that the speaker owns a car, but barring some reason to doubt that she does, they are likely to add that content to CG in order to help process her utterance. When they do so, we say that interlocutors have *accommodated* the speaker's presupposition.[8] Matters would likely be different had she said,

I'm sorry I'm late, but my camel was being ornery.

In the next chapter we will explore ways in which presupposition may be exploited for manipulative purposes. Until then, let us observe the rich variety of techniques a modern speaker might employ for getting a message across: you might assert it outright, assert something else that entails it, conventionally implicate it, conversationally implicate it, or (pragmatically) presuppose it. Each of these approaches will of course bring with it distinctive nuances, including advantages and pitfalls. Nonetheless, now that we have the tools for distinguishing these different approaches to communicating a single content, it is hard not to be impressed with our ingenuity, both in our role as agents who mean

---

8. See Simons (2006) for further discussion of presupposition accommodation.

things, as well as in our role of addressees who in most cases effortlessly discern what speakers mean.

6.4. Explicature

In this chapter we have worked so far with a certain picture of the relation of what is said to what is implicated. According to this picture, the former is determined by the literal meaning of the sentence used, fleshed out if necessary by means of a "saturation" process that assigns intensions to any indexicals the sentence might contain, and resolves any lexical or structural ambiguities. If the utterance of that sentence also generates a conversational implicature, this is due to the speaker's intentions in saying what she did, together with her exploitation of conversational norms and her expectation of common understanding among herself and interlocutors of the state of the conversational project.

Carston (2002) and Carston and Hall (2012) argue that this picture is unrealistic. Their main reason for this view is that in a wide variety of cases, what a speaker says (and not just what she speaker-means), is even more context-sensitive than we have acknowledged so far. In support of this view, they offer examples like the following. Assume a weeping child approaches his mother with an obviously skinned knee. The mother remarks:

6.15. You're not going to die.

On the standard truth-conditional account of the truth conditions of 6.15, it will be true only in the case that there is no future time at which the child will perish. If this is not the case, then the child's mother has said something obviously untrue. Perhaps we can accommodate this within the Gricean model by analogy with the hyperbole case discussed earlier ('The line was a mile long'), in which the speaker says something patently true but still succeeds in getting her message across by means of a conversational implicature. Other cases are less easily accommodated to this model:

6.16. To buy a house in San Francisco, you need money.

A speaker of 6.16 is likely not making the trivial claim that to buy a house in that city, one needs to have some money rather than none. Rather, she is likely claiming that one needs a substantial sum of money, presumably more than would be needed in most other housing markets. Carston and Hall (2012) deny that this further content is conversationally implicated by the utterance of 6.16. Instead, they in effect propose that 6.16 is best understood as

6.17. To buy a house in San Francisco, you need money*

where 'money*' expresses an ad hoc concept, that is, a concept that is defined for the occasion and in a way that is driven by a general tendency to construe one another's utterances as cooperative contributions to the conversations in which they occur.[9] (Here, 'money*' might express the concept of being, say, at least $1,000,000.)

Carston and Hall argue for a general phenomenon of *modulation*, in which a great many expressions conventionally express only a semantic template that is then specified more fully upon their utterance. If this viewpoint is correct, then many sentence types (even those free of indexicality and ambiguity) express contents that are far removed in meaning from what speakers might use those sentences to say. On such an approach, pragmatic phenomena are considerably more pervasive than is suggested by the picture bequeathed to us by Grice.

6.5. Study Questions and Suggestions for Further Reading

Study Questions

1. Please come up with your own examples of indexical expressions beside those mentioned in Section 6.2. Once you have done that, please formulate a rule that describes the character of each one you have found.

2. Would you expect the conversational maxims set out in Box 6.1 to be cross-culturally universal or to vary from one culture to another? In your answer, please bear in mind the possibility of communication becoming pointless if, for example, no speakers respect the Maxim of Quality.

3. In Section 6.3, we mentioned the possibility of nonconventional, nonconversational implicature. Please try to describe a case falling into this category distinct from the example given in 6.3.

---

9. Carston and Hall work within a framework known as Relevance Theory, which is a descendant of the Gricean approach. According to Relevance Theory, interlocutors make and interpret utterances guided by a presumption of Relevance, which prioritizes the maximization of informational content while minimizing processing costs. For further discussion, see Wilson and Sperber (2004).

4. People often assert what the logical empiricists would have called tautologies: "A deal is a deal"; "War is war"; and so on. In so doing, they seem to be conveying a more substantive message than the tautological form of their utterance suggests. What might that more substantive message be?
5. Please review the logical constants discussed in Chapter 3, particularly disjunction. There we noted that everyday conversational practice suggests a divergence between disjunction defined as a connective and its associated truth table, and 'or' as used in everyday talk. Can the concept of implicature help explain this divergence without our having to posit an ambiguity, or a more complex set of truth conditions for sentences of the form 'A or B'? Please explain your answer.

Further Reading (with recommended [*] items for instructors)

Kaplan (1989)* is a classic discussion of indexicality. Reimer (1991) investigates different semantic and pragmatic approaches to demonstratives. Lewis (1979)* is a highly influential study of the concept of conversational context and the explanatory uses to which it might be put. DeRose (1992) is an influential discussion of contextualism as it applies to knowledge attributions, and Ichikawa (2017) contains many state-of-the art essays on epistemic contextualism. Cappelen and Lepore (2005) criticize a variety of forms of contextualism. Grice (1989)* is the canonical text for the theory of implicature. Horn (2004) and Bianchi (2013) are succinct introductions to the topic, while Davis (2013) treats it in greater detail. Geurts (2012) is a lucid and insightful discussion of implicatures generated by interaction with the Quantity maxim. Green (2019) defends a minimalist approach to so-called quantity implicatures. Soames (1989) and Simons (2006) are excellent introductions to semantic and pragmatic presupposition, respectively. Bach (1999) attacks Grice's notion of conventional implicature, arguing that it is an amalgam of quite different phenomena. Carston (2002) and Carston and Hall (2012) articulate and defend the utility of the notion of explicature; Bach (1994) discusses a related notion that he terms "implicature."

References

Bach, K. 1994. "Conversational Implicature." *Mind & Language* 9: 124–162.
Bach, K. 1999. "The Myth of Conventional Implicature." *Linguistics and Philosophy* 22: 327–366.

Bianchi, C. 2013. "Implicating." In *Pragmatics of Speech Actions*, edited by M. Sbisa and K. Turner, 107–142. Berlin: de Gruyter.

Cappelen, H., and Lepore E. 2005. *Insensitive Semantics: A Defense of Semantic Minimalism and Speech Act Pluralism*. Oxford: Blackwell.

Carston, R. 2002. *Thoughts and Utterances: The Pragmatics of Explicit Communication*. Oxford: Blackwell.

Carston, R., and Hall, A. 2012. "Implicature and Explicature." In *Cognitive Pragmatics*, edited by H.-J. Schmid, 47–84. Berlin: de Gruyter.

Davis, W. 2013. "Implicature." In *Stanford Encyclopedia of Philosophy*, edited by Edward Zalta. https://plato.stanford.edu/

DeRose, K. 1992. "Assertion, Knowledge, and Context." *The Philosophical Review* 111: 167–203.

Garcia-Carpintero, M. 2008. "Singular Thought and the Contingent A Priori." *Revue Internationale de Philosophie* 62: 79–98.

Geurts, B. 2012. *Quantity Implicatures*. Oxford: Oxford University Press.

Green, M. 2019. "Assertion, Implicature & Speaker Meaning." *Rivista Italiana di Filosofia del Linguaggio* 13: 100-115..

Grice, P. 1989. *Studies in the Way of Words*. Cambridge, MA: Harvard University Press.

Horn, L. 2004. "Implicature." In *The Handbook of Pragmatics*, edited by L. Horn and G. Ward, 3–29. Oxford: Blackwell.

Ichikawa, J. 2017. *The Routledge Handbook of Epistemic Contextualism* (New York: Routledge).

Kaplan, D. 1989. "Demonstratives." In *Themes from Kaplan*, edited by J. Almog, J. Perry, and H. Wettstein, 481–564. Oxford: Oxford University Press.

Lewis, D. 1979. "Scorekeeping in a Language Game." *Journal of Philosophical Logic* 8: 339–359.

Reimer, M. 1991. "Demonstratives, Demonstrations, and Demonstrata." *Philosophical Studies* 63: 187–202.

Simons, M. 2006. "Foundational Issues in Presupposition." *Philosophy Compass* 1: 357–372.

Soames, S. 1989. "Presupposition." In *Handbook of Philosophical Logic*, Vol. IV, edited by D. Gabbay and F. Guenthner, 53–616. Dordrecht: D. Reidel.

Stalnaker, R. 1975. "Pragmatic Presuppositions." Reprinted in his *Context and Content*, 47–62. Oxford: Oxford University Press.

Wilson, D., and Sperber, D. 2004. "Relevance Theory." In *The Handbook of Pragmatics*, edited by L. Horn and G. Ward, 607–632. Malden, MA: Blackwell.

CHAPTER 7

....

Despicable Discourse

Chapter Overview

This chapter discusses issues shared by Philosophy of Language, Social and Political Philosophy, and Feminism. We begin with an account of ways in which linguistic practices may be unjust and in which individual speakers may behave inappropriately. We then turn to loci of language use that have generated the most interest around injustice and malfeasance: slurs, certain epithets, and generics. Thereafter we examine ways in which patterns of injustice in one's community may prevent one from performing the speech acts one sets out to perform. We close with some brief suggestions for how one might combat these forms of communicative injustice.

7.1. Injustice and Malfeasance in Language

We have thus far worked with a picture of communication in which every speaker is free to speak her mind and to contribute to a conversation as an equal of others, subject to the typically short-lived norms created by the kind of conversation in which she is engaged. This is, of course, an idealization: local etiquette might dictate that those who have made a certain religious pilgrimage have higher conversational priority than do others, or that the words of elders carry more weight than do those of the young. Again, and more to our purposes in this chapter, a speaker may be marginalized due to malfeasance of her own or to that in her linguistic milieu. In either case such marginalization may be dramatic, effected in part by someone's racist, sexist, or other discrimi- natory remarks, or it may develop subtly in ways that make it difficult to detect both for participants and observers. Philosophers of language have in the last two decades begun to pay attention to such harmful pat- terns of language use, and in the process they have illuminated territory between our field and the fields of Social and Political Philosophy, as well as Feminist Philosophy.

How might a speaker come to be marginalized due to her own malfeasance? If, following the approach of the last two chapters, we construe some speech acts as aimed to contribute to an ever-evolving conversational common ground (CG), we may then ask whether condi- tions might arise in which a speaker's contributions fall under a shadow of suspicion. This may occur as a result of her history of abusing the norms that govern speech acts such as assertion, either through lying or a tendency to make statements that may be sincere but that are not justified by the evidence that was available to her. You may be famil- iar with speakers prone to unjustified statements on particular topics rather than across the board: friends who are good judges of movies but who overrate new musicians; others are reliable about directions but hopeless in their views about how long it takes to get to various desti- nations. Someone who acquires a reputation for unreliable assertions, either through a pattern of lies or of unjustified claims, either generally or on particular topics, will find it more difficult than it would normally be to have his proffered contributions accepted into CG. Instead, his interlocutors may treat his statements as manifest events in the sense of that expression introduced in Chapter 5, but not extract the content of those statements for the sake of updating CG. It is now CG that Helmut claimed that P, but we are not inclined on that basis to accept P as well without independent corroboration. This phenomenon is captured in Aesop's fable of the boy who cried wolf.

Another form of malfeasance emerges when we consider speakers who use what we might call charged language. In this class we find pe- joratives, which are derogatory terms that denigrate people and other objects such as nonhuman animals; slurs, which are derogatory terms that denigrate people in light of their membership in a certain group; and certain types of negative epithet, which characterize objects (and, commonly, people) as having undesirable qualities in a way that makes it difficult for others to challenge. We discuss these cases in more detail in the next section.[1]

We begin to discern injustice in linguistic usage—which we shall term 'communicative injustice'—when some aspect of language use deprives a person of opportunities or powers for reasons irrelevant to the extent to which she might merit them, and in ways traceable to the choices of others. It may be unfair that I lack the physical attributes needed to be a professional cyclist, but such a limitation need not be unjust since it need not be due to anyone's choice. By contrast, if I do possess those competitive features but am excluded from the cycling team due, say, to my skin color, then that is likely a case of injustice. The distinction carries over to language. A disability for which you cannot be blamed might cause cognitive limitations preventing you from fully contributing to conversations of which you would like to be a part. This is unfair, but not unjust. Further, and as we will see in more detail later, some uses of language can subordinate a person in the sense of leading others to view her, consciously or unconsciously, as being below a standard expected for human beings along such dimensions as intelligence, hygiene, trustworthiness, or manners. Any of these effects might deprive the subordinated target of opportunities she would otherwise be entitled to pursue. Likewise, if my attempts to contribute to a conversation are hindered not by any pattern of malfeasance on my part, but instead result from others' construal of me as unreliable due to my skin color, sexual orientation, gender, physical disability, or religious affiliation, then that is likely a case of communicative injustice. The reason is that I have been kept off, or at least kept on the margins of one or more conversational "teams" for reasons not relevant to my qualifications for membership.

Keeping in mind that language is a crystallization of countless choices made by individual speakers, we also find that it contains unjust features that have been conventionalized. As we shall see later, charged language can support communicative injustice by marginalizing individuals as well as whole groups. In this category we also find sexist or racist sayings such as 'x throws like a girl,' 'x wears the trousers around

---

1. Nothing in principle rules out the possibility of slurring something other than a person, such as a nonhuman animal or institution. Observe also that the "charge" in charged language need not be negative. If we could coin an antonym of 'slur' it might be 'valor,' which would refer to expressions that valorize individuals in light their membership in a certain group.

here,' 'x has gone off the reservation,' 'x was blacklisted'; or the use of pronouns of one gender to refer to both men and women, particularly 'he' in sentences ostensibly intended to cover both men and women, as in 'He who laughs last laughs best'; as well as words such as 'crazy' and 'insane' to refer to certain types of behavior or situation. These are examples that would seem to justify describing a particular language as having racist, sexist, ableist, or homophobic elements.

7.2. Slurs and Epithets

One need not read far into the news headlines before encountering reports of people who have been fired from their jobs or attacked on social media for using a racial or ethnic slur or some related form of derogatory language. While many current societies place considerable value on freedom of speech, most of them also limit it for such reasons as public safety. Similarly, in many countries the use of hate speech is a punishable offense.[2] Hate speech often contains "charged" language such as slurs and certain types of epithet. But how can words, even when used in an illocutionary act, have such power as to provoke some societies to punish their users? To begin to see why such a response might have a basis, let us examine some accounts of slurs.

Slurs: Pejoratives are expressions, normally either nouns or verbs, that are conventionally designed to denigrate individuals. 'Slut' for instance, when used to refer to a woman, denigrates a woman by suggesting that she has numerous sexual partners, and that such promiscuity is inappropriate.[3] Other words have over time shed their requirement of expressing a more general property: 'bastard' referred in the past to those who were born out of wedlock, and given that extramarital sex was frowned upon by church and other authorities, the word's use carried a negative suggestion about the person so described. However, we can now call someone a bastard without committing ourselves to any conclusions about the marital condition of his mother at his birth.

---

2. The *Encyclopedia Britannica* characterizes hate speech as "speech or expression that denigrates a person or persons on the basis of (alleged) membership in a social group identified by attributes such as race, ethnicity, gender, sexual orientation, religion, age, physical or mental disability, and others" (https://www.britannica.com/topic/hate-speech).

3. Notice that one meaning of 'stud' is to refer to a man who is promiscuous, but the term is not a slur.

Instead, the term is now most commonly used to impute to its referent a tendency to behave badly regardless of parentage. (Some usages of the word violate this pattern, as we see in the phrase 'poor bastard.')

Though they are both pejorative terms, 'slut' differs from 'bastard' in that even in embedded contexts other than quotation, the former's use in a speech act commits the speaker to the view (expressed roughly) that a woman merits condemnation if she has numerous sexual partners.[4] Consider

> I wonder if she's really a slut.
> Some people I've talked to have suggested that she's a slut.
> If she's a slut, she'll eventually pick up an STD.

If I illocute (and not merely locute) any of these sentences, I seem to commit myself not to the view that a certain person has numerous sexual partners, but rather to the more general view that a woman's having numerous sexual partners merits condemnation. Recalling our discussion in Chapter 6 of the 'projection problem' for presupposition, we may accordingly call a word like 'slut' a *projectile*: regardless of how deeply embedded it is under logical constants, attitude verbs, and the like, its use in a speech act commits the agent performing that act to the pejorative content conventionally associated with that word. We do not find a parallel phenomenon with 'bastard':

> I wonder if he's really a bastard.
> Some people I've talked to have suggested that he is a bastard.
> If he's a bastard, he'll probably have few friends.

I can illocute any of these three sentences without committing myself to a view about what kind of behavior merits condemnation. This is reason to think that while 'bastard' and 'slut' are both pejorative terms, the latter differs from the former in being a slur as well.

Slurs are among the most emotionally and politically charged expressions in any language. With the right intonation, facial expression,

---

4. Such a commitment is incurred even if the speaker does not intend to undertake it. However, it should be noted that subgroups within a larger language community can and often do reclaim slurs for their own purposes such as empowerment. For instance, supporters of the SlutWalk movement might come to use 'slut' in a nonpejorative way, perhaps in part to highlight the right of women to have as many sexual partners as they see fit. Over time, such a movement may imbue the word 'slut' with a new conventional meaning such that it is no longer a slur.

and other stage setting, we can use most any word or expression slur-ringly. But think of words like 'kike,' 'breeder,' 'faggot,' 'wog,' or the 'N word.' Such words typically have a so-called neutral counterpart: Jew, heterosexual, homosexual, South Asian, and Black, respectively. Also, some slurs are more offensive than others: some of the above five words are highly offensive, while a contemporary British person is unlikely to be much perturbed at being called a 'Pom' by an Australian, for instance.[5]

How do slurs convey this further, often more offensive, message? Each of the aforementioned five slurs goes beyond its neutral counter-part in suggesting that there is something about being Jewish, hetero-sexual, and so on, meriting condemnation. Although in general one can commit oneself to an attitude without expressing it, it also seems that slurs express, or are at least expressive of, derogatory attitudes toward both the individual, if any, to whom she refers in a particular speech act and the associated group. What is more, we also tend to feel that slurs are apt to subordinate the individuals to whom they refer as well as the groups that they single out for abuse: those who are slurred tend to be thought of and treated as lesser than others in some way, for instance as less clean, less reliable, or even as less than human. Another feature of slurs that speakers sometimes note is that being part of a conversation in which a slur is used can make one feel complicit in the promotion of certain derogatory attitudes unless one explicitly objects to the use of that term. It may be observed as well that speakers sometimes slur people they know not to fall within the extension of the slur's neutral counterpart.

Summing these features of slurs together, then, we have:

1. Slurs are projectiles.
2. Slurs incur commitment to a derogatory attitude toward the asso-ciated group and, by implication, any targeted individual(s).
3. Slurs tend to express the attitude mentioned in (2).
4. Slurs tend to subordinate the associated group, and, by implica-tion, any targeted individual.

---

5. There are also words that seem to fall in a grey area between slurs and the more general category of pejorative. It is not clear whether 'geezer' just means something like 'elderly person who tends to be eccentric or cantankerous' (and so is just a pejorative), or whether it goes beyond this to function as a projectile expressing an ageist prejudice (and so would be a slur).

5. Being part of a conversation in which a slur is used tends to produce a sense of complicity.
6. One can slur a person even if he does not fall within the extension of the slur's neutral counterpart, and even if one is aware that he does not do so.

Theories of slurs differ on how best to explain these phenomena. Some approaches are purely semantic, in that they attempt to account wholly for slurs' behavior in light of a characterization of their semantic content. A proponent of the semantic approach, Hom (2008), asks us to imagine first of all that p^*_1, p^*_2, p^*_n, are a series of discriminatory treatments of individuals, such as a policy of refusal to let them patronize certain businesses, or passing them over for promotions in the workplace; that d^*_1, d^*_2, d^*_m, are a series of negative properties derived from racist, sexist, ablest, and so on, ideology; and that NPC* is the semantic value of a slur's neutral counterpart. Then on this view, a slur's semantic content may be codified as:

Ought to be subject to p^*_1 + ... + p^*_n because of being d^*_1 + ... + d^*_n all due to being NPC*.

For instance, the semantic value of a slur such as 'Mick' may be captured with:

(I) Ought to be subject to exclusion from positions of high social status, etc., because of being unreliable and prone to alcoholism, altercations, etc., all due to being Irish.

Hom points out that his analysis is not one that we would expect ordinary speakers to be able to articulate on their own. The fact that an elucidation such as given in (I) is not self-evident to an ordinary speaker is thus no objection to that elucidation.

An immediate problem confronts this semantic approach, however, for such an approach would predict that so long as they occur embedded, the use of slurs should not be thought offensive. For instance, where 'I' abbreviates the long condition above, there is nothing offensive about asserting any of the following:

If she is I, then we live in an unjust society.
George thinks that Sean is I.
Katherine thinks Gwyneth is I, but actually she's Welsh.

Yet, as we have observed, slurs are projectiles.

Following Hom in pursuing a semantic approach to slurs, Bach (2018) offers what he terms "loaded descriptivism." Bach's proposal gains some inspiration from an analogy with nonrestrictive relative clauses such as we find in the following sentence.

7.1. Astrid, who is Armenian, has strong opinions about genocide.

A speaker who asserts 7.1 asserts that Astrid has strong views about genocide; she might also assert, or at the very least undertake assertoric commitment[6] to, the further proposition that Astrid is Armenian. Bach tells us that slurs behave in a similar manner:

> Loaded descriptivism says that the meaning of a slur has two components, a categorizing part and a supplementary evaluative part, which is a function of the categorization. For example, the semantic content of "kike" includes the property of being Jewish and the property of being contemptible in virtue of being Jewish. (2018, p. 64)

However, Bach tells us, unlike nonrestrictive clauses, the supplementary evaluative part is not given separate linguist expression, but is rather "loaded into the slur." Bach shows that his proposal has virtues that some competitor theories lack. However, it also inherits the central challenge faced by Hom's semantic approach. The reason is that if all we know is that a slur expresses two contents, that information will be no basis for predicting that it will function as a projectile. After all, a speaker may express any number of contents while remaining neutral on their truth or applicability more generally. This is not to say that loaded descriptivism could not be modified to yield the appropriate prediction, but it will not do so as it stands.

In an attempt to overcome these difficulties with purely semantic approaches, authors such as Schlencker (2007) advocate a view of slurs as triggering presuppositions in the sense of that notion explored in Chapter 6. Such a suggestion might come as a surprise. After all, while it is fairly intuitive that a speaker who says "Even Emir can lift the barbell" takes it for granted that if anyone can be expected to have trouble

---

6. We may understand assertoric commitment as follows: if A asserts p, and p entails q, A is committed to q, even though she may not have asserted it. Further, her commitment to q is assertoric rather than under some other illocutionary modality, as we may observe if we imagine instead that A had conjectured p. (In that case, A would have undertaken "conjectural" commitment to q.) See Green (2016) for fuller discussion of the distinction between assertion and assertoric commitment.

with that weight, it would be Emir; it is less intuitive that a speaker who says, "Susan's new boyfriend is a Mick" presupposes that there is something questionable about Irish people. More decisive, however, is the fact that slurs have projectile properties that we would not predict given the thesis that they are presupposition-triggering words. For the latter normally do not project out of attitude clauses. For instance, in "George thinks that even the old mastiff can make it over the hurdle," we ascribe to George the view that an elderly mastiff can make it over a certain hurdle, and that if any dog can be expected to have trouble doing so, it will be him. However, we need not ourselves endorse either of these propositions just by virtue of ascribing what we have to George. Similarly, you might enter a department store and ask a clerk, "Could you please point me to the millenary department— if there is one?" In so speaking you are making clear that you're not presupposing that the store has a millenary department. However, a similar distancing effort will not work for slurs: "I wonder if there are any breeders at the party—which is not to suggest that there's anything wrong with being heterosexual." Such an utterance would seem to show that the speaker does not understand 'breeder' or some other word in her utterance.[7]

Instead of a purely semantic or presupposition-involving approach, we might try to account for the properties of slurs in pragmatic terms. On one version of this approach, indicative sentences containing slurs have no truth conditions, but speakers who illocute them express negative attitudes such as contempt toward an individual or group of individuals. To be illuminating, such a view would need to elucidate the notion of expression at play. Also, the denial of truth values to indicative sentences containing slurs might seem heavy handed in a way reminiscent of the semantic approach to presupposition. For instance, Richard argues for such a denial as follows:

> Imagine standing next to someone who uses S as a slur. ... The racist mutters that building is full of Ss. Many of us are going to resist allowing that what the racist said was true. After all, if we admit its truth, we must believe that it is true that the building is full of Ss. And if we think that, we think that the building is full of Ss. We think, that is, what and as the racist thinks. (Richard 2008, p. 13)

---

7. See Cepollaro (2015) for a defense of a presupposition approach to slurs in response to objections such as that offered in the text.

This line of thought does not establish its conclusion. The reason is that we can think what the racist thinks without thinking as he thinks, and we may do so while accepting that the building in question is full of S's. Indeed, we might say to the racist, "Strictly, what you say is true, but I object to your way of putting it."

A more promising approach to slurs starts with the proposal to adhere to a straightforward semantics, according to which slur-containing indicative sentences have the same truth conditions as their neutral counterparts. But we refine the approach by noting that slurs also have a pragmatic dimension. For as we have noted, slurs, in light of their projectile properties, are among the few expressions in language that Frege-Geach considerations, mentioned in Chapter 2 in discussing emotivism, leave untouched. This suggests a view on which at the pragmatic level, slurs are words whose job is to express attitude A toward an individual or group of individuals on account of their being of type T. As we have seen, an artifact expresses attitude A just in case it is designed, though not necessarily intended, to convey information about that attitude. Such an artifact might also express a particular agent's attitude, but need not always so do; in the latter case we have an artifact that is expressive without expressing the agent's attitude. Further, the attitude in question might be a negative one, to the effect that members of a certain group are unclean, violent, untrustworthy, or in some other way merit denigration.

What attitude or attitudes are expressed by a slur? Some authors such as Jeshion (2013) contend that all slurs express an attitude of contempt. This, however, seems unduly narrow. Instead, it would appear that a slur could express an attitude of disgust (like the Rwanda-Rundi metaphorical slur 'iyenji,' translatable as 'cockroach'), revulsion, or hatred, or in principle any of a variety of other negative attitudes such as bemusement. Also, we may invoke this idea of attitude expression to account for the ability of slurs to subordinate certain groups. Being on the receiving end of an expression of contempt, disgust, hatred, or a like attitude is not a pleasant experience. It tends to corrode one's sense of self-worth. So, too, being an observer of such an expression tends to make one, unless you put up some resistance, share that negative attitude, if only by virtue of the process of emotional contagion.[8] Sensitive observers for this reason stand a good chance of not just noticing that

---

8. For more on emotional contagion, see Hatfield, Cacioppo, and Rapson (1993).

attitude, but "catching" it as well. Further, attitude expressions tend to be directed toward a certain target. Whether or not that target is present, it is prone to being perceived as having a lower status in the view of others. Supported by a fuller account of the notion of expression, a more flexible "expressivist" view of slurs can improve on Jeshion's approach while retaining its explanatory virtues.

Epithets: In the previous section we mentioned nonrestrictive relative clauses (NRRCs), which grammarians distinguish from restrictive relative clauses (RRCs). The latter occur in such constructions as

7.2. The horse that is brown is a swift runner.

Here the relative clause 'that is brown' restricts the scope of the referent so that the addressee only considers brown horses as possible items being discussed. By contrast, consider the sentence

7.3. The horse, which is brown, is a swift runner.

Here the parenthetical clause 'which is brown' serves not to restrict the reference of the noun phrase to horses of a certain color, but instead to make a further claim about the referent, namely that it is brown. This difference is not substantial for many purposes, but in some cases it affects what the speaker is committing herself to. If the speaker uses 7.3 in a speech act, including those in which 7.3 is embedded within the scope of a larger sentence, she is still committing herself to the proposition that the horse being discussed is brown. Such a strong claim cannot be made of 7.2.

NRRCs have in some cases been categorized as generating conventional implicatures. This is not accurate if we are to adhere to the constraint that conventional implicature expressions do not contribute to what is said: surely, part of what the speaker says in 7.3 is that a certain horse is brown. However, NRRCs are similar to conventionally implicating words in that they have a tendency to present their content as uncontroversial and so meriting accommodation in the sense of that term we discussed in the last chapter.

The distinction between RRCs and NRRCs is useful to bear in mind as we consider epithets. This is because epithets gain some of their power from the fact that they function in a way similar to NRRCs. For instance, I once saw a van with the following words painted on the side:

7.4. This vehicle runs on clean natural gas.

The default interpretation of 7.4 is not that the vehicle runs on the kind of natural gas, among many that are available, that is clean. (Contrast 7.4 with 'This vehicle runs on purple natural gas.') Rather, it is that natural gas is clean, and that the vehicle runs on it. A gloss of this would thus be with a NRRC, as in

> 7.5. This vehicle runs on natural gas, which is clean.

We said earlier that NRRCs tend to present their content as noncontroversial and so to be accommodated into CG. The result is that 7.4 is readily used to get the reader to accept that natural gas is clean without that proposition being presented as a focus of scrutiny. The environmental merits of natural gas need not detain us here. However, consider such sentences as:

> Lying Letitia is exaggerating again.
> That scumbag in the Lexus took my parking spot.
> Charles the Round Mound of Rebound Barkley is a great athlete.

We may of course challenge a speaker who proffers one of these for entry into CG. However, if we do so in what may be the most natural way, such as with "No, she isn't/he didn't/he isn't," that will leave it unclear whether we are accepting or rejecting the claim that Letitia is a liar, that the Lexus driver is a scumbag, and so on. We would need to go to greater effort to clarity that we are rejecting this latter claim by, for instance, saying, "No she isn't exaggerating, and she isn't a liar either." Since, however, in conversation as elsewhere, we tend to default to a path of least effort, we may not put in the extra labor needed to make our position clear. The result is that the suggestion that Letitia is a liar may sneak into CG. Knowing this, a speaker may use epithets in order to insinuate a content into CG in such a way that it comes to be presupposed by interlocutors. As we will see later, a similar "slipperiness" in generic sentences makes them difficult targets for conversational challenges.

7.3. Generics

When we introduced the concept of quantification in Chapter 3, we noted the variety of ways in which quantified sentences are used. For instance, while 'The whale is a mammal' could be used to make a remark about a particular whale, it may also be used to say that all whales are mammals. So, too, 'A whale is a mammal' might be used to make a purely existential claim, or it could instead be universal in scope.

In a like manner, generic sentences (which are general sentences lacking explicit quantificational expressions) show considerable heterogeneity. 'Tigers have stripes' is normally used to say that most tigers have stripes, or at least that normal tigers do: it is no objection to this latter claim that we know of a tiger that, due to a genetic anomaly, was born stripeless. But you may also have heard some such remark as 'Mosquitoes carry West Nile virus.' This sentence may be true, but if it is, then that will be in spite of the fact that only a small portion of mosquitoes (no more than 1 percent) carry this virus.

We will not try to develop a semantic and/or pragmatic theory of generic sentences to make sense of this bewildering variety. Instead, it will suffice for our purposes to note that scholars have taken interest in recent years in the ability of generics to serve as a window into how speakers conceptualize their social world. Consider such generic sentences as

> Asians are good at math.
> Men don't ask for directions.
> Women are emotional.

A speaker who asserts one of these sentences may merely be making a statistical generalization. However, more often it would seem that a speaker who asserts one of these is invoking a (possibly mythical) underlying nature that accounts for the property in question such as being good at math, unable to ask for directions, or emotional. Wodak et al. (2015) call these "essentialized kinds," which are kinds of entity that we take to share an essential but unobservable or difficult-to-observe property that accounts for a wide range of observable phenomena.

These alleged essential properties of various groups might have little or no basis in reality; instead, our interest here is in the ability of generics to shed light on how speakers represent their social worlds to themselves. Such representations may rarely be consciously scrutinized, and yet they may still play a large role in our expectations about and consequent behavior toward one another. What is more, claims invoking essentialized kinds are difficult to challenge in everyday conversation. One reason is that a speaker who asserts, for instance, that Asians are good at math, is not going to be refuted by a response pointing out that some Asians are not: we all know there can be outliers. They might not even feel their claim to be challenged by someone who points out that students of Asian descent are no better at math than the general population of students. The reason is that the speaker might insist that there may have been a factor in the population studied preventing the manifestation of the underlying Asian nature. Such hard-to-challenge, and thus hard-to-shake, assumptions about social groups might in turn be self-fulfilling in two ways. First of all, the well-documented phenomenon of confirmation bias[9] predicts that we will tend to focus on behavior that confirms our stereotypes and ignore behavior that might challenge it; second, expectations of caregivers, educators, and others might lead members of the stereotyped groups to behave in conforming ways. If girls are made to understand that they are more emotional than boys, many of them might conform to that expectation as a means to social survival. We see this in the phenomenon of stereotype threat.[10]

At this point it is possible to discern a common theme shared by slurs and generics that invoke essentialized social kinds. The reason is that, like many generics, slurs may be understood as invoking a putative underlying nature of certain groups (Asians, heterosexuals, women, etc.) in order to derogate them. Speakers express contempt toward members of a certain group on account of their imputed negative characteristics such as lack of hygiene, proneness to violence, or obsession with money. In the minds of speakers, these negative characteristics would seem to flow from an underlying nature or essence that all members of a certain group allegedly share. Generics and slurs, then, go hand in hand, the former supporting the latter in that speakers who use slurs will often assume an underlying essence applying to members of the slurred group and justifying their derogation of that group.

7.4. Silencing, Distorting, and Subordinating

Another way in which living in an unjust society can affect one's role as a communicator brings up the phenomenon known as illocutionary silencing. Recall from Chapter 5 Austin's tripartition among locutionary, illocutionary, and perlocutionary acts. A person may, of course, be silenced at the locutionary level as a result of being gagged or being in a situation in which it is too noisy to be heard. These cases, although disturbing in their own right, are distinct from those that have generated

---

9. See Oswald and Grosjean 2004 for discussion of confirmation bias.
10. See Spencer, Logel, and Davies (2016) for further discussion of stereotype threat. Carnaghi and Bianchi (2017) discuss the phenomenon of group labeling.

recent philosophical interest. For perhaps finding oneself in an unjust milieu makes one unable, or at least hard-pressed, to perform the speech acts one would like to be able to perform. Betting, for instance, can only occur if one's addressee accepts the bet. For this reason, a bet cannot take place unless it receives the appropriate uptake. As a result, if due to prejudice you have been categorized as a person who does not honor her bets, then your attempt to bet with others will misfire.

Similarly, Langton (1993) and Langton and Hornsby (1998) consider cases that pertain to women's illocutionary freedom in societies that tend to marginalize and objectify them. Let us assume that members of a certain society, and particularly men in that society, see women as primarily objects of entertainment and sexual gratification. Included in this is the tendency to see women who resist romantic overtures from men as being coy or even flirtatious. In such a situation, a man who makes a romantic overture to a woman might get a reply such as "No" or "I'm not interested." However, the man's expectations about women lead him to see such apparent refusals as veiled invitations to further overtures. The result, Langton and Hornsby argue, is that a woman's attempt to resist such overtures will misfire with such an audience. Like the proffered bet that is not accepted, the attempt to refuse a romantic advance will not succeed in being the illocutionary act that its producer intends it to be. In both cases we have illocutionary rather than locutionary silencing, and in the refusal case this occurs due to forms of injustice in the social milieu.

An assumption implicit in this line of reasoning is that refusing is relevantly similar to betting in requiring uptake on the part of any addressee. That assumption may, however, be disputed. As Bird (2002) points out, a homeowner might place in plain view in her yard a sign with the words "Beware of dog." If a careless intruder fails to see the sign, or sees it and ignores it, and is subsequently maimed by the homeowner's dog, he could not reasonably complain that he was not warned. Instead, the homeowner could point out that her placing of the sign did serve as a warning to all who entered the yard whether or not they noticed it. This example suggests that warning is a speech act that does not require uptake on the part of others. So long as the message is made suitably discernible, a warning has been issued.

Might refusing and warning be similar in this respect? For all that Langton and Hornsby have established, it may still be that the speech act of refusing can be performed without being understood as such by any addressees. Instead, on this alternative hypothesis, so long as the speaker has succeeded in manifesting her intention not to accept the man's overture, his incomprehension would be regrettable, and reflect poorly on him, but may not cause the woman's act to misfire.

It seems, then, at best controversial to claim that the speech act of refusal requires audience uptake on pain of misfiring. Skepticism is also reasonable for other proposals that we encounter in the literature on illocutionary silencing. Kukla (2014), for instance, imagines a case in which a woman has been appointed as foreman in a factory. In that role, she issues what she takes to be orders to workers under her authority. However, due to their sexist views about women, most of these workers construe the foreman's speech acts as suggestions rather than orders, and thus as remarks that they are free to honor or ignore as they see fit.

As with the Langton/Hornsby approach, that of Kukla depends on a controversial assumption. In particular, one might doubt that others taking your utterance to be the performance of a particular speech act is sufficient for it being that speech act. I might, for instance, utter an indicative sentence with the force of a conjecture, and so am only prepared to defend it provisionally if challenged; I am not presenting P as something I know to be true. If others take me to be putting forth P with the force of assertion, they have misunderstood not what I have said but how I meant it. Accordingly, their taking my utterance to be an assertion does not make it one. So, too, in Kukla's case, the new foreman's utterance is, so long as she makes her intentions manifest, an order and not a suggestion, and if other employees take her to be doing otherwise, they are in error.[11]

We have considered two ways of conceptualizing how patterns of prejudice in one's social milieu can compromise one's attempt to perform the speech acts one sets out to perform. Each of them rests on an assumption that may be challenged. Might a third route prove less controversial? Perhaps an approach focusing on differences of degree rather than kind might be of assistance here. That is, recalling that speech acts

---

11. A speaker might make a remark, such as "You're rather eccentric," intending it to be a criticism, while her addressee takes it instead as a compliment. Does this show that speakers do not always have final say on the force of their utterances? Perhaps, but it may only show that sometimes hearers can willfully misconstrue the force of others' remarks for certain, sometimes laudable, purposes.

depend in part on the intentions with which an agent does what she does, we may also observe that intentions require, as a matter of conceptual necessity, a minimal associated belief. I cannot intend to do X when I am certain that I have no prospect whatever of succeeding in doing X. This may explain why I cannot intend to travel to the moon by flapping my arms, or, if today is Tuesday, why I cannot intend to make it the case that yesterday was not Monday. We may crystallize these insights with a principle linking intention and belief:

> Intention/Belief Principle: One can only intend to do X if one believes that one is capable of doing X. Further, the more difficult doing X appears, the more difficult it will be to form the intention to do X.

If something like the I/B Principle is correct, we may begin to discern why living in a prejudiced social milieu puts some speakers up to a higher standard than others in order to achieve their illocutionary aims. Even if I know that my utterance is an order, if I also have doubts that it will be grasped as such, I will have difficulty intending it to be correctly understood. On this approach, disempowered speakers are not silenced, but may well have intentions, and thus their corresponding illocutions, distorted by unjust institutions in which they find themselves.

7.5. Paths to Amelioration

We have considered a number of ways in which communicative injustice might occur. Is there something that speakers wishing to challenge such injustice might do? A number of strategies present themselves.

- First, a gut-check never hurts: Do you ever give members of particular groups less credence or conversational "air time" due to that group membership? Men who are accused of "mansplaining" may be guilty of such behavior toward women and other groups who are under-represented in certain professional domains. You might also catch yourself being particularly critical of certain speakers, challenging claims they make or asking for clarification with more frequency than you do with others. Consider leveling the conversational playing field. One place to start would be to determine if you harbor any implicit bias. (The Implicit Association Test may easily be found online.)
- Learning about the history of slurs is often illuminating. See, for instance, Kennedy (2003) and Nunberg (2018).

- We do sometimes find ourselves in a conversation in which another speaker uses a slur or a dubious generic. Particularly in the case of slurs, some have contended that even as listeners we may come to feel complicit in the slurring. One way to combat this is to politely but firmly challenge the speaker's objectionable use. Langton (2018) discusses this as a case of what she calls "blocking."
- Consider Nunberg's (2019) proposal for the use of gender-neutral pronouns. Making the switch may seem awkward at first, but with time you may find the new ways of speaking becoming second nature.

7.6. Study Questions and Suggestions for Further Reading

Study Questions

1. The examples of slurs we discussed in this chapter were all nouns. Can you think of any other parts of speech, such as verbs, that are slurs?
2. We sometimes carry on private monologues in our own heads. Even if you agree that it is inappropriate to use a slur in public, might it nevertheless be appropriate to use a slur in this arena of "inner speech"? Please explain your answer.
3. Does the observation that slurs are projectiles serve as a counterexample to Davidson's Autonomy Thesis? Please explain your answer.
4. Have you ever felt that a speech act that you (or someone that you knew) were attempting to perform was being silenced in the sense of that term used by Langton and Hornsby, or distorted in the sense of that term used in this book? Please explain the situation.
5. If you could reform language, would you get rid of generics? Why or why not?

Further Reading (with recommended [*] items for instructors)

Hom (2008) is an influential semantic approach to slurs. Jeshion (2013) approaches them as vehicles of expression of contempt. Williamson (2009) defends a view of slurs in terms of conventional implicature, and Maitra addresses many aspects of so-called subordinating speech. Sosa (2018) is a collection of recent papers on the topic (including Bach 2018), and DiFranco

(2015) provides an accessible survey of literature on the topic. Leslie (2008) and Wodak, Leslie, and Rhodes (2015) are excellent introductions to generics. Langton (1993) and Hornsby and Langton (1998) are the origin of the "silencing" argument; Bird (2002) offers a strong challenge to that argument. Saul and Diaz-Leon (2017) discuss some of the topics of this chapter in the broader context of feminist philosophy of language.

References

Bach, K. 2018. "Loaded Words: On the Semantics and Pragmatics of Slurs." In *Bad Words: Philosophical Perspectives on Slurs*, edited by D. Sosa, 60–76. Oxford: Oxford University Press.

Bird, C. 2002. "Illocutionary Silencing." *Pacific Philosophical Quarterly* 83: 1–15.

Carnaghi, A., and Bianchi, M. 2017. "Group Labeling." *Oxford Research Encyclopedia of Communication*. https://oxfordre.com/communication/view/10.1093/acrefore/9780190228613.001.0001/acrefore-9780190228613-e-435?rskey=4KNMRt&result=1

Cepollaro, B. 2015. "In Defense of a Presuppositional Account of Slurs," *Language Sciences* 52: 36–45.

DiFranco, R. 2015. "Pejorative Language." In *Internet Encyclopedia of Philosophy*. https://www.iep.utm.edu/pejorati/

Fricker, M., and Hornsby, J., eds. 2000. *The Cambridge Companion to Feminism in Philosophy*. Cambridge: Cambridge University Press.

Green, M. 2016. "Assertion." *Oxford Handbooks Online*, ed. D. Pritchard. New York: Oxford University Press.

Hatfield, E., Cacioppo, J., and R. Rapson (1993) *Emotional Contagion*. Cambridge; Cambridge University Press.

Hom, C. 2008. "The Semantics of Racial Epithets." *Journal of Philosophy* 105: 416–440.

Hornsby, J., and Langton, R. 1998. "Free Speech and Illocution." *Legal Theory* 4, no. 1: 21–37.

Jeshion, R. 2013. "Expressivism and the Offensiveness of Slurs." *Philosophical Perspectives* 27: 307–335.

Kennedy, R. 2003. *Nigger: The Strange Career of a Troublesome Word*. New York: Vintage Books.

Kukla, R. 2014. "Performative Force, Convention, and Discursive Injustice." *Hypatia* 29: 440–457.

Langton, R. 1993. "Speech Acts and Unspeakable Acts." *Philosophy and Public Affairs* 22, pp. 293–330.

Langton, R. 2012. "Beyond Belief: Pragmatics in Hate Speech and Pornography." In *Speech and Harm: Controversies over Free Speech*, edited by I. Maitra and

M. McGowan, 72–93. Oxford: Oxford University Press. doi:10.1093/acprof:
oso/9780199236282.003.0004

Langton, R. 2018. "Blocking as Counter-Speech." In *New Work on Speech Acts*,
edited by D. Fogal, D. Harris, and M. Moss, 144–164. Oxford: Oxford
University Press.

Leslie, S. J. 2008. "Generics: Cognition and Acquisition." *Philosophical Review*
117: 1–49.

Maitra, I. 2012. "Subordinating Speech." In *Speech and Harm: Controversies over
Free Speech*, edited by I. Maitra and M. McGowan, 94–120. Oxford: Oxford
University Press.

Nunberg, J. 2018. "The Social Life of Slurs." In *New Work on Speech Acts*, edited
by D. Fogal, D. Harris, and M. Moss, 237–295. Oxford: Oxford University
Press.

Nunberg, J. 2019. "Even a Grammar-Geezer Like Me Can Get Used to Gender-
Neutral Pronouns." *National Public Radio*. https://www.npr.org/2019/08/06/
744121321/even-a-grammar-geezer-like-me-can-get-used-to-gender-
neutral-pronouns

Oswald, M. and Grosjean, S. 2004. "Confirmation Bias." In *Cognitive Illusions:
A Handbook of Fallacies and Biases in Thinking, Judgment, and Memory*,
edited by R. Pohl, 79–98. New York: Academic Press.

Richard, M. 2008. *When Truth Gives Out*. Oxford: Oxford University Press.

Saul, J., and Diaz-Leon, E. 2017. "Feminist Philosophy of Language." In *The
Stanford Encyclopedia of Philosophy*, edited by Edward Zalta. https://
stanford.library.sydney.edu.au/entries/feminism-language/

Schlenker, P. 2007. "Expressive Presuppositions." *Theoretical Linguistics* 33:
237–245.

Sosa, D., ed. 2018. *Bad Words: Philosophical Perspectives on Slurs*. Oxford:
Oxford University Press.

Spencer, S., Logel, C., and Davies, P. 2016. "Stereotype Threat." *Annual Review of
Psychology*, 67: 416–437.

Williamson, T. 2009. "Reference, Inference, and the Semantics of Pejoratives."
In *The Philosophy of David Kaplan*, edited by J. Almog and P. Leonardi,
137–158. Oxford: Oxford University Press.

Wodak, D., Leslie, S.-J., and Rhodes, M. 2015. "What a Loaded Generalization:
Generics and Social Cognition." *Philosophy Compass* 10, no. 9: 625–635.

CHAPTER 8

Artful Language

Fiction, Metaphor, Irony, and Jokes

Chapter Overview

This chapter explores some common ground between Philosophy of Language and Aesthetics. We begin with the role of language in fictional discourse such as we find in novels and short stories: are the authors of such works performing speech acts, pretending to do so, or engaging in an entirely different activity? From fiction we look to similes and metaphors in an effort to shed light on how they work, and why speakers and their audiences often find them so compelling. Next, while irony is a pervasive feature of everyday conversation, we will consider some open questions as to how best to understand it. Finally, we offer some brief remarks about jokes, but Mae West will have the last word.

8.1. Fictional Discourse

While some of the pictures we draw manually are for the sake of conveying information or capturing a memory, others are intended at least in part for aesthetic appreciation. We or someone else might enjoy contemplating them not just as configurations of line and color but also as representations of something distinct from themselves. As Aristotle remarked,[1] we take pleasure in seeing one thing as another: we may see a few lines in charcoal as a fish, or splotches of watercolor as clouds. Doing so engages our imagination: we imagine, in looking at these lines, that we are seeing a fish, and in looking at those splotches, some clouds.

Language engages the imagination as well and provides many of the pleasures we get from pictures we make with our hands. We can "paint" a visual picture of a scene by describing it vividly ("A cracked blue teacup stood on the table next to an oscillating fan"), enabling hearers to construct an image of their own. This can occur in the course of our recounting an event we experienced, or as we tell a story of our own making. Consider a short story such as J. D. Salinger's "A Perfect Day for Bananafish." In that story, the author tokens these two sentences:

8.1. She was a girl who for a ringing phone dropped exactly nothing. She looked as if her phone had been ringing continually ever since she had reached puberty.[2]

In one sense, Salinger did not mean 8.1: we could not accuse him of lying if we find out that he knew no one conforming to the description given. Yet in another sense, Salinger intended to write this particular sentence, and probably gave considerable thought to its exact formulation. That would seem to justify saying that he meant what he wrote. How may we reconcile these two seemingly incompatible lines of thought?

The tools we have developed in previous chapters can help us make some headway here. First of all, when Salinger writes 8.1 as part of his story, he is not putting his utterance up to the standards of veracity we would expect for assertions. This fact might tempt us to suggest that authors of fictional works are liars. However, with some exceptions, liars intend their audiences to believe what they are saying. Yet if we could ask Salinger if he intended to deceive anyone, I suspect he would reply with some bemusement and remark instead that he only intended for us to imagine what he is saying to be so, not to believe it. Further, it

---

1. "Imitation is natural to man from childhood, one of his advantages over the lower animals being this, that he is the most imitative creature in the world, and learns at first by imitation. And it is also natural for all to delight in works of imitation ... though the objects themselves may be painful to see, we delight to see the most realistic representations of them in art" (*Poetics*, 1448^b).

2. J. D. Salinger, "A Perfect Day for Bananafish," *The New Yorker*, January 31, 1948.

does not seem that an author can deceive a reader simply by getting her to imagine something. After all, you can imagine the most outlandish things without thereby falling into error. Nevertheless, Salinger surely gave careful consideration to what he wanted his readers to imagine. Here we begin to see the sense in which he did not, and the other sense in which he did, mean what he wrote.

We make as if to bake and eat pies when we play "mudpies," and when we gaze at the sky on a clear night, we might make as if to see a dipper or a bear. Perhaps, as Searle (1975) suggests, authors of fiction similarly only make as if to perform speech acts. On this approach, Salinger in the lines quoted earlier was only pretending to tell his readers about a woman named Muriel. But as Currie (1985) observes, while making as if to perform a speech act seems a fair characterization of what many (though not all) actors do when delivering their lines, it seems not to capture all of what an author does. The reason is that it leaves out the author's role in overtly stipulating what is true in her or his story. When Salinger writes the two lines comprising 8.1, he also makes it the case that Muriel is someone who for a ringing phone drops exactly nothing. Currie also argues that the author of a fictional work performs a speech act in the technical sense of that term introduced in Chapter 4. On Currie's analysis, the author writes sentences such as those in 8.1 with the intention that the reader imagine that the contents of those sentences are true. According to this approach, authors of fictional works perform speech acts generated by reader-directed intentions. In light of our conception of speech acts as acts of the sort that can be performed by saying and speaker-meaning that one is doing so, we may characterize the appropriate saying as

8.2. I hereby stipulate that it is to be imagined that Muriel was a girl for whom a ringing phone ...

This characterization does not imply that the author of fiction says$_{thin}$ 8.2, but, rather, only that it is an elucidation of the intentions with which she utters the words she does. Also, unlike assertions, conjectures, and guesses, stipulations such as these are not, at a local level, held to a standard of adhering to what is actually the case. (I will return in a moment to explain the qualification.) Instead, for the most part, if an author intentionally tokens a sentence S, then S is true in her story.[3] That will be

---

3. There will be exceptions to this general rule. For instance, if an author tokens 'not-P' on page 11 of a novel, and then explicitly contradicts it with a tokening of 'P', we might be unsure what is true in the story.

so whether or not making S part of the story is the best authorial choice that could have been made, and whether or not readers are happy to find out that S is true in the story.

Another reason to see authorial utterances as speech acts is that they share many features with everyday discourse. For instance, an author and her readers share a common ground (CG) that develops as the story progresses.[4] This is attested by the fact that the author can felicitously presuppose material that has been mentioned in the story previously or is a plausible inference from something else that has been mentioned. Further, just as in real life we sometimes hear conflicting accounts of events that have occurred, so, too, some works of fiction require a more nuanced picture accommodating numerous narrators all created by one author. These narrators might tell incompatible stories, forcing the reader to decide who is more reliable, or, if that cannot be determined, to keep track of multiple CGs.

Some storytelling is sheer fantasy, and so it is beholden to few norms. However, the broad notion of fiction encompasses works that are expected to correspond in large part to actual fact. The extent to which they are so expected is determined in large part by the genre in which the fictional work is to be placed. So-called New Journalism departs from known fact only marginally in order to fill in narrative details that are difficult or impossible to know. We see this in works like Truman Capote's *In Cold Blood*. Historical fiction is permitted more liberty with facts, so long as the main features of the historical period in which the story is set are respected. At the other extreme are genres such as magical realism in which readers can have no objection to stories in which, for instance, a character lives a long life while subsisting on the dirt she finds on the floor of her hut.[5]

Whether we accept the pretense theory or the speech act theory of fiction, it seems clear that authors of fictional works are not typically making assertions when they token indicative sentences. However, in some cases we do find authors writing lines in works of fiction that seem

---

4. Even before reading the first lines of a novel or short story, a reader from the same culture and historical epoch will share considerable CG with the author; when culture, epoch, and so on differ between reader and author, interpretive difficulties can mount, and in some cases readers will find the fictional work largely unintelligible. Try reading *Gilgamesh* with no one to help provide background!

5. The example is drawn from G. Márquez (1970) *One Hundred Years of Solitude* (New York: Harper & Row) a quintessential work of magical realism.

to call out for interpretation as things that the author is putting forth as true. In *Howard's End*, for instance, E. M. Forster writes,

> When we think the dead both treacherous and absurd, we have gone far towards reconciling ourselves to their departure.[6]

Given the context, it is plausible to conclude that Forster is putting forth this sentence as true. Accordingly, it sometimes happens that individual sentences in a work of fiction are asserted rather than pretend-asserted or being put forth as to be imagined. Furthermore, we often react to what we know to be a work of fiction in such a way as to suggest that we take that work to be in a broad sense offering a picture that is not true to the world. Suppose you read a story in which a character who has been struggling with heroin addiction for many years wakes up one morning and decides never to use the drug again. Suppose further that in the story, the character indeed never uses heroin again, and never even feels the temptation to do so. It would be natural to be dissatisfied with such a story given how implausible it is on account of contradicting well-known facts about addiction. (We might briefly wonder whether the author intended for it to fit into another genre, such as satire.) Alongside that dissatisfaction would likely be the feeling that the author is offering a picture of what is involved in getting over addiction that is not true to the facts of that disease. If the author were to defend her story by reminding us that it was just a story, we might reply that in that case, it was a mediocre one at best.

Let us not, then, overestimate the gap between fiction and nonfiction. Even the former may be put up to norms of accuracy. Further, we sometimes take ourselves to learn from our experience with works of fiction such as novels and short stories. One important means comes via our learning what someone else's experience is like. To get a better grasp of this notion and its relevance to language, we now turn to the topics of simile and metaphor.

8.2. Similes and Metaphors

In a simile, we say$_{thin}$ that two things are alike in some respect:

  8.3. She was as fast a softball pitcher as anyone in the league.
  8.4. Listening to that speech was about as interesting as watching paint dry.
  8.5. Your love is like a hurricane.

---

6. E. M. Forster ([1910] 2000), *Howard's End* (New York: Penguin Books), 85.

Some similes are hyperbolic in that the speaker is making a stronger claim than she likely feels is true. 8.4 is probably a case of this sort, since although the speech in question might have been quite boring, it probably was not as bad as watching paint dry, which could take hours or days. 8.3, by contrast, we readily imagine as being meant literally. In this case it is plausible that the speaker not only says$_{thin}$ 8.3 but also says$_{thick}$ it.

By contrast with the first two examples, the third says only that two things are alike without specifying the respect in which they are so. Let us call this a bare simile. This case raises a prima facie problem of interpretation since any pair of objects are similar in some respect. For instance, your left nostril and the Battle of Poltava share the property of not being identical with the number 37. Thus if someone tells you that your left nostril is like the Battle of Poltava, you could reply by agreeing that, strictly speaking, what they say is true. However, in typical cases, when someone says that A is like or similar to B, she is relying on her addressee to discern the relevant or salient respects in which they are similar. Well, returning to example 8.5, what properties do hurricanes have that could possibly be like a person's love? Presumably they are such properties as being overwhelming, dangerous, and perhaps destructive. Although hurricanes also bring damaging winds and low barometric pressure, we would not expect the speaker in this case to have these properties in mind, not least because human beings generally do not produce such effects.

The producer of the hurricane simile is using imagery, and she may be doing so with a purpose of conveying how she feels about the addressee's affections. Perhaps those feelings are something like the following: when I contemplate your love toward me, I feel how I would feel if I were to see a hurricane heading toward me: scared, overwhelmed, helpless, perhaps even doomed. On this way of conceiving similes, then, some of them have an expressive role in that the speaker designs them to show others how she feels.[7] From what we have learned about expressive communication, we should expect such an utterance to fall within the realm of organic meaning without rising to the level of speaker meaning.

When we compare A with B, we often also do so with our "folk" preconceptions about B's in mind. Thus when we describe our finicky toddler as eating like a bird, we probably have in mind finches and

---

7. Green (2017) develops the connection between simile, metaphor, and expression in further detail.

parakeets, though martial eagles eat entire monkeys and ferruginous hawks eat whole rabbits. Interpreting a simile tends to invoke nominal essences, that is, characteristics that we believe to be essential to a kind of object, rather than characteristics that are in fact essential to it.

As with fictional discourse, then, similes often trade in imagery. Similes also share with fiction the property that they can be assessed as being better or worse. Given that any two objects are alike in some respect, however, it would seem that strictly speaking, every bare simile is true. A more useful dimension of assessment than truth may instead be aptness. A question might be apt not, of course, because it is true (since being true is a property that questions could not have), but rather because trying to answer it will lead us in a useful direction: doing so might help us solve a practical problem or direct our attention to interesting theoretical possibilities. So, too, a simile might be apt because of the useful work it does for speaker, addressee, or both. Our hurricane simile earlier, for instance, might have enabled the speaker to express his ambivalent feelings about another's affections. That in turn may help the addressee to empathize with the speaker. Aptness in cases such as this would appear, then, to concern what is emotionally illuminating.

Other similes have a less expressive and more cognitive role, but they may still be assessed in terms of their aptitude. Researchers who study the development of human culture like to describe cultural evolution as being like a ratchet.[8] Because ratchets are tools that can be readily tightened but can only be loosened with difficulty, this simile helps students to understand cultural-evolutionary processes. In this case, calling a metaphor apt appears to be a reference to its intellectually utility.

Philosophers have spent vastly more effort on understanding metaphors than they have on similes. Some of the reasons for their doing so may have to do with the fact that at least construed literally, metaphors tend to say things that are, strictly speaking, absurd. Consider, for instance:

8.6. Devin's life has become a train wreck.
8.7. The new CFO blew the lid off that meeting.

The only things that can become train wrecks are trains, and meetings do not have lids. Yet neither of these remarks is terribly difficult for hearers to understand. How do they manage it?

---

8. See for instance Tenny, Call and Tomasello (2009).

Alexander Bain writes, "What is only implied in the Metaphor is distinctly expressed in the Simile" (Bain 1890, p. 170). Bain does not tell us what kind of implication he has in mind, and we now know that implication may come in many forms. One form that such implication may take is ellipsis. Ben Franklin once said in his *Poor Richard's Almanac*:

> Laws too gentle are seldom obeyed; too severe, seldom executed.

Here Franklin is using ellipsis in the material after the semicolon. We may for this reason report him in indirect discourse as having said that laws that are too severe are seldom executed. So, too, one construal of Bain is as holding that metaphors are elliptical similes. That does not itself tell us whether the simile in question is bare or nonbare. In either case, however, brief reflection will reveal that our practice of indirect discourse does not support the ellipsis construal. How, for instance, might we report what the speaker of 8.7 said? We might try

> George said that the new CFO did something similar to blowing the lid off the meeting.

It seems unlikely that George would agree that he had said this. Furthermore, even if he did say this, the fact is not likely to help elucidate 8.7, since we still must agree that meetings lack lids.

Another interpretation of Bain's use of "implied" would invoke our notion of conversational implicature. This is the approach to metaphor championed by Grice (1989) and Searle (1979). On this approach, recalling that conversational implicatures may be triggered by an apparent violation of a conversational norm, we note that metaphors such as 8.6 and 8.7 appear to violate the Maxim of Quality. Given that such violations cause addressees to search around for another speaker-meant content beyond what is said$_{thin}$, we may suppose that speakers fasten upon such a content as part of their charitable attempt to preserve the assumption that the speaker is adhering to the Cooperative Principle. In response to the train wreck metaphor, for instance, we suppose that the speaker is conversationally implicating that Devin's life has met with insurmountable obstacles in some way, such as those concerning addiction, financial problems, or difficulties with the law.

Researchers typically distinguish between "live" and "dead" metaphors. The former are metaphors of the sort that we just exemplified. By contrast, dead metaphors are words or expressions that were once live but that have become part of the literal meaning of those words or expressions. 'Up against the wall' wears its metaphorical origins on its sleeve, but now it is a phrase that seems literally to mean something like 'in a difficult situation.' Similarly for 'over the moon' and 'between a rock and a hard place.' It will not take long for you think of many dead metaphors in one or more of the languages you speak. One useful feature of these dead metaphors is that if a hearer has not heard the phrase before, she may be able to discern its meaning from the imagery that the words invoke. After all, it is clear that being between a rock and a hard place is a difficult situation to be in whether the hard place in question is another rock, a wall, or a something similar. Also, there is surely a nebulous area between live and dead metaphors in which a conventional meaning is beginning to attach to a phrase used metaphorically, but it has not done so completely. Perhaps we may call these *moribund metaphors*.

One traditional view has it that when a speaker offers a (live) metaphor, her words take on momentary, new meaning that enables the remark to make sense (and possibly even be true) after all. This view is associated with Beardsley (1962), who defends what he calls the Verbal Opposition theory of metaphor. To illustrate his idea, Beardsley quotes the English cleric Jeremy Taylor's (1613–1667) remark that "virginity is a life of angels, the enamel of the soul." Perhaps when he used it in the seventeenth century, Taylor's use of "enamel" as an adjective applying to "soul" had little precedent. However, Beardsley contends that we are nonetheless able to comprehend this metaphor, and he suggests that we do so by attaching what in Chapter 1 we called a "nonce-sense" to this term. Beardsley writes,

> Yet to speak of virginity as the enamel of the soul is surely to say ... that it is a protection for the soul, and that it is the final touch of adornment on what is already well-made. Thus this metaphor does not merely thrust latent connotations into the foreground of meaning, but brings into play some properties that were not previously meant by it. (1962, p. 303)

Beardsley seems to be assuming that in order to account for how Taylor's metaphor works, we must understand him to saying that virginity is a final adornment on what was already well-made. That may only be possible if "enamel" takes on a nonce-sense.

Later authors rejected the assumption that metaphorists say anything beyond the literal meaning of their words. Davidson (1978) famously challenges the "meaning shift" theory of metaphor, claiming instead that in verbal metaphors, speakers' words do not take on novel meanings:

> metaphors mean what the words, in their most literal interpretation mean, and nothing more. (1978, p. 32)

For Davidson, instead, it is not that metaphors are successful (when they are) because they say anything new beyond the literal meaning of the words used; rather, they succeed by such means as causing listeners or readers to form images (visual, tactile, etc.) and contemplate them, as well as attend to likenesses. Thus when we are told that virginity is the enamel of the soul, we appreciate the metaphor by forming images, or seeing certain people in a particular light, as opposed to grasping a particular proposition distinct from that expressed by the words Taylor used.

One question we might raise for Davidson concerns the process by which live or moribund metaphors become dead. A natural thought would be that by the time a metaphor has become moribund, speakers are using it to express a fairly definite thought, distinct from that expressed by the words' literal meaning; then over time that thought ossifies into a literal meaning, at which time the metaphor may be pronounced dead. However, such a picture seems precluded by Davidson's noncognitivist approach, as it is difficult to see where the thought that undergoes ossification would come from.[9]

Another question for Davidson's approach stems from the case of "twice-true" metaphors. Some utterances are literally true but also seem to be carrying a further metaphorical suggestion beyond that. Camp and Reimer (2006, p. 856) offer the example of "Jesus was a carpenter." A speaker may in uttering this sentence intend not only to convey information about Jesus' profession but also to suggest something of wider significance. Davidson might reply that this latter information is only suggested or intimated. In discussing T. S. Eliot's poem "The Hippopotamus," Davidson acknowledges that "The poem does, of course, intimate much that goes beyond the literal meaning of the words. But intimation is not meaning" (p. 41).

To this last remark we might reply, "It depends." In particular, whether intimation rises to the level of speaker meaning will depend on the metaphorist's intentions. For a more banal example than that of Eliot, imagine that emerging from a business meeting with some prospective clients, you remark happily, "Getting that contract was low-hanging fruit."

---

9. See Reimer (1996) for further discussion.

Even if that metaphor has never been uttered before, I may reasonably conclude that you are informing me that you got the contract with little difficulty. To account for such phenomena, we may wish to follow approaches to metaphor that see them as forms of conversational implicature. Searle (1979) and Grice (1989) offer theories along these lines. As you will recall from Chapter 5's discussion of implicature, theories of this sort will see the metaphorist as speak-meaning something beyond her words' literal meaning. This in turn means that the speaker's utterance will produce an apparent violation of the Cooperative Principle or one of its associated maxims. Once this has occurred, the addressee searches for a charitable interpretation of what the speaker might have meant. So long as that interpretation falls within the ambit of what the speaker intended, there will have been a successful case of metaphorical communication.

Camp and Reimer (2006) object to the implicature view of metaphor on several grounds, one of which is that some metaphors involve sentences that seem quite true, and so do not appear to violate conversational norms. Their example is Donne's "No man is an island." However, the defender of the implicature theory could reply that even though this sentence is true, its utterance still violates a conversational norm; after all, it is usually uncooperative to go about preaching trivialities. So, just as 'A deal is a deal' is usually used to convey more than a sentence of the form 'A is A,' likewise, Donne is doing more than denying that human beings are identical with land formations surrounded by water.

A more compelling objection to the implicature theory that Camp and Reimer raise is that it will deny that a metaphor's significance goes beyond what the speaker intended it to be; for speaker meaning is, as we have seen, a creature of intentions. But some metaphors are novel, striking, and intriguing, and cause hearers to have quite disparate responses to them. The art historian Walter Pater in *Studies of the Renaissance* wrote,

> To burn always with this hard, gemlike flame, to maintain this ecstasy,
> is success in life.

While Pater's image is striking, we may doubt that he intended to convey with it a particular proposition distinct from whatever those words mean. Instead, it seems more plausible that Pater was offering up an image that readers may reflect on and draw insight from at various times and in various ways as they see fit. Davidson's approach seems plausible for such cases. By contrast, the implicature theory may be useful for the less esoteric metaphors involving low-hanging fruit and blowing the lid off meetings. Perhaps, then, given their heterogeneity, we should not take for granted that one theory will work for all verbal metaphors.

In fact, we may discern a range of types of metaphor, some of which are quite open-ended like Pater's while others are more prosaic like that of the example of low-hanging fruit. Loosely correlating with this range will be a range of increasingly precise sets of intentions on the part of the speakers who produce them. Corresponding to the most open-ended metaphors will be comparatively bare intentions in which the speaker intends little more than to share an image. In intermediate cases (such as the hurricane simile turned into a metaphor) will be metaphors produced with an expressive aim but possibly nothing beyond that: the speaker hopes her image will help her addressee know how she feels, but nothing more. In the most prosaic cases, the metaphor is readily interpretable, and perhaps sufficiently familiar to hearers that they might even be tempted to characterize the speaker as having said$_{thick}$ that (e.g.) getting the contract was easy. If no one theory accounts for all these cases, that might just attest to the ingenuity with which we use imagery in our speech.

8.3. Irony

Another common means by which speakers communicate with artistry is verbal irony. Irony occurs in the course of much satire, and it may be directed toward things as disparate as individuals, governments, codes of conduct, and sensibilities. In the eighteenth century, the essayist Jonathan Swift chose to lampoon the harsh policies of the British toward the Irish by suggesting that the overpopulation problem in the latter country be solved by cannibalizing its children:

> I do therefore humbly offer it to public consideration that of the hundred and twenty thousand [Irish] children, already computed, twenty thousand may be reserved for breed... That the remaining hundred thousand may at a year old be offered in sale to the persons of quality and fortune through the kingdom, always advising the mother to let them suck plentifully in the last month, so as to render them plump and fat for a good table. A child will make two dishes at an entertainment for friends; and when the family dines alone, the fore or hind quarter will make a reasonable dish, and seasoned with a little pepper or salt will be very good boiled on the fourth day, especially in winter. (Swift 2008, p. 7)

Swift is here using irony to suggest that the British are so barbaric that they might just take such a proposal seriously. Yet in spite of its ubiquity in everyday speech as well as more high-profile communication such as Swift's, irony is not easily analyzed.

Traditionally, irony has been divided into situational, dramatic, and verbal types. Situational irony may be understood as any state of affairs in which an action or event constitutes a severe violation of an established or ostensible norm. This is what we have in mind in describing it as ironic that the President of Mothers Against Drunk Driving (MADD) got arrested for driving while intoxicated. Dramatic irony is found in fictional stories such as plays or movies, and it occurs when a character is unaware of something that the audience is aware of. Closer to our concerns here is verbal irony. In response to your dropping your wallet into a fast-flowing river, I might remark, "Nice job!" Here I do not speaker-mean that you did a nice job in acting as you did; if anything, I mean the negation, namely that you did a lousy job. This type of observation is what motivates theories of irony dating back as far as Quintilian (c. 35–c. 100 AD), who characterized it as a figure of speech in which something contrary to what is said is to be understood.[10]

This "inversion" theory of verbal irony was accepted for centuries. It does not, however, apply to all cases. Suppose I have had a serious cycling accident and am lying immobile and bleeding in the middle of a road. A passerby approaches and asks, "Do you need some help?" I reply, "How could you tell?" Since it is not clear what the negation of a question could be, but it is clear that my question is ironic, this would seem to be a counterexample to the "inversion theory" or irony.

We will return to theories that accommodate cases such as this one. For now, note that Grice follows the inversion theory and, as you might imagine, aims to understand irony as a form of conversational implicature. On this approach, by asking "How could you tell?" in the previous case, I am only making as if to ask a question, and am instead speaker-meaning that the passerby's question is a silly one. Although Grice does seem to accept the inversion theory, that view is not integral to his approach, and we might consider a liberalization of it that does not insist on inversion. On the other hand, Grice is committed to the view that verbal irony is a form of speaker meaning, and we might question this commitment. Must the ironist be seen as speaker-meaning a

---

10. For references to this and related classical sources, see Vlastos (1987).

content distinct from her words? Perhaps the ironist is doing something different, such as echoing an attitude that she wants to lambast, or pretending to adopt such an attitude in order to express disdain toward it.

These two possibilities point to the two most influential theories of irony today, the echoic theory and the pretense theory. The former starts with the observation that speakers sometimes echo the words of others without committing themselves to those words' content. A student of limited technical skills enters my office to announce that he has proved a notoriously difficult logic theorem. I reply:

> You proved the theorem. What axioms did you use?

Here I have echoed the student's claim to have proved the theorem without asserting it. Wilson (2006) and Wilson and Sperber (2012) use this notion of echoic uses of language to motivate their approach to verbal irony. For them, when someone goes outdoors into yet another drizzly English day, she might remark to her companion,

> Lovely weather we're having for this time of year, don't you think?

In so doing, the speaker seems to be echoing a typically English sentiment that tries to make the best of things no matter how miserable. At the same time, however, she is also expressing disdain for such an attitude. Wilson uses the term "dissociative attitude" to encompass attitudes such as skepticism, mockery, disdain, or rejection. She then writes,

> the main point in typical cases of verbal irony … is to express the speaker's dissociative attitude to a tacitly attributed utterance or thought (or, more generally, a representation with a conceptual content, for instance a moral or cultural norm), based on some perceived discrepancy between the way it represents the world and the way things actually are. (2006)

We may be concerned that this construal of verbal irony has wider scope than it should, treating as ironic cases that are not. Let us return to the example of the President of MADD under arrest. Suppose you happen to be passing the scene where the President has been apprehended and observe her failing miserably on a sobriety test. Knowing that she is President of the local MADD chapter, you remark, "That's ridiculous!" Here you are expressing a dissociative attitude, and doing so toward a tacitly attributed thought (a thought typically espoused by this President, to the effect that she is a paragon of sober diving), and you are doing so on the ground of a perceived discrepancy between the way this thought represents the world and how things are. Nevertheless, you are not being ironic at all.

The other best-known theory of verbal irony is cast in terms of pretense. The suggestion here is that the ironist pretends to possess an attitude, perspective, or sensibility, and in the course of doing so, she also express an attitude toward the point of view thus feigned. Sperber (1984, p. 131) objected to earlier versions of the theory that pretending to adopt a point of view, no matter how absurd, is not itself enough for irony. (Just imagine an actor portraying Torquemada at the height of his inquisitorial powers.) A contemporary defender of the pretense theory, G. Currie (2010, pp. 156–158), responds by suggesting that the pretense must also draw attention to what he calls a target, which need not be identical to the point of view that the ironist pretends to have. An actor playing a U.S. Government official reciting alternative facts would be making as if to possess a perspective, and at the same time to express an attitude toward that perspective, by taking the government official as her target. (She might do so by dressing up as such an official, talking like one notable such figure known for her penchant for recitations of alternative facts, and so on.)

Currie, then, distinguishes between targets and points of view. One might adopt a point of view that is not identical with the target of one's irony. For instance, someone might be moderately unreliable in calculating tips at restaurants, and I might ironize him by pretending to calculate a wildly implausible tip amount compared to the price of our meal. Here the point of view is that of someone incompetent in simple mathematics, while the target is someone with genuine but limited competence. The relation could also be reversed: the target might be outrageously incompetent in some way, and we ironize it by pretending to be mildly incompetent.

Currie formulates his version of the pretense theory as follows:

> what matters is that the ironist's utterance be an indication that he or she is pretending to have a limited or otherwise defective perspective, point of view, or stance F, and in so doing put us in mind of some perspective, point of view, or stance (which may be identical to F or merely resemble it) which is the target of the ironic comment. (2010, p. 157)

Note first that the phrase "pretending to have a limited perspective" is ambiguous between two readings. It might refer to cases in which the speaker pretends to have a perspective that is in fact limited, though she does not present this perspective as being limited. Or the phrase might refer to cases in which the speaker pretends to have a certain perspective that she also presents as being limited. The first disambiguation would seem to be too weak for Currie's purposes, since unless the speaker does something to indicate the limitations of the perspective mimicked, no irony will result. Accordingly, we will adopt the second construal of Currie's words.

In some cases, the pretense involved in an ironic utterance comes with a genuine illocution. One may be ironic while making an assertion and not just a faux assertion, for instance. I have a neighbor who is extremely fastidious about his lawn: he is forever raking, mowing, weeding, and fertilizing. Suppose that on walking past it one day I notice that a leaf has fallen onto the lawn from a nearby tree. I immediately call him on the phone and say,

> George, I just saw a leaf on your lawn. I thought you'd want to know.

Here I am asserting, and not pretending to assert, that there is a leaf on George's lawn. I am also being ironic, drawing attention to the absurd lengths to which George goes to care for his lawn. Here I am pretending that George's fastidiousness is so extreme that he would appreciate being told about that leaf.

As with the echoic theory, we may doubt whether the pretense theory covers a sufficiently wide range of cases. In so-called verisimilar irony, a speaker makes a remark that she believes true while managing to be ironic all the same. Suppose a mother enters her child's messy bedroom and remarks,

> I just love it when my kids keep their rooms spotless!

This is an ironic remark, but the speaker does indeed love it when her kids keep their rooms clean, even if that rarely occurs. Is the mother pretending not to notice the mess in this case, and thus pretending to have a limited perspective? That seems unlikely.

8.4. Jokes

In addition to meaning some of what we say ironically or metaphorically, we also sometimes mean what we say as a joke. Making a joke does not of course ensure that anyone will find what you say funny, but most likely you are attempting to elicit someone's enjoyment, even if that enjoyment is at the expense of a third party. More specifically, jokes are utterances put forth *as* humorous whether or not they are in fact humorous. In paradigmatic jokes, we generally do not speaker-mean what we say, but intend others to appreciate what we say by finding it humorous. Producing a laugh is nice work if you can get it, but we often find jokes humorous that do not elicit our laughter.

Cicero wrote,

> The most common kind of joke is that in which we expect one thing and another is said; here our own disappointed expectation makes us laugh. (Cicero 1942)

A disappointed expectation does not, however, seem enough to produce laughter or even to make us find something humorous. You might be expecting a speaker to say one thing, but she says something else; a more likely response on your part would be surprise. A further ingredient of much humor seems to be that in some cases in which our expectations are disappointed, this fact reveals something absurd or at least questionable about them. As an example, Mae West once said,

> Marriage is a great institution, but I'm not ready for an institution.

The first conjunct of this sentence activates our concept of the institution of the modern family. But the second conjunct activates our concept of an institution as a place where the mentally ill are cared for. That switch does produce a disappointed expectation but also does more than that: it also forces us to acknowledge that marriage can be constricting for some even to the point of driving them mad. To find West's quip humorous is, I suggest, to be compelled to view one of your own confidently held beliefs as questionable.

On this way of understanding some types of jokes, we stand to learn about ourselves from what we find humorous. Thus while a good joke can have aesthetic value, it also offers epistemic value to sensitive audiences. Indeed, this dual aesthetic/epistemic character of some jokes is shared with irony and metaphor. The ironist attempts to present a perspective or sensibility as being defective, and thus hopes to show us how not to think or feel about a situation. Further, in spite of the heterogeneity of metaphors, at least one important class of such cases shows us how things appear from the speaker's point of view and thus puts us in a position to empathize with them. The aesthetic and epistemic value of these uses of language would seem, in fact, to reinforce each other.

8.5. Study Questions and Suggestions for Further Reading

Study Questions

1. Please try to think of a work of fiction from which you feel you learned something. Please explain what it is that you learned, and how the work of fiction conveyed that knowledge to you.
2. Consider the view of metaphors as elliptical similes. How might one invoke our practice of indirect discourse to provide evidence against that view?
3. How might one tell whether a metaphor (or seeming metaphor) is alive, dead, or moribund?
4. Please explain the main features of the echoic and pretense theories of verbal irony. Which of these two theories do you find most persuasive? Please give your reasons for that preference.
5. Recalling the account of speech acts given in Chapter 5, please take a stand on whether jokes should be considered a type of speech act, being sure in the process to support your position with one or more reasons.

Further Reading (with recommended [*] items for instructors)

Stock (2017) defends a compelling theory of authorial intentions in fiction from a Gricean perspective. Davidson (1984)* is a classic defense of a "noncognitivist" approach to metaphor. Camp and Reimer (2006) provide a useful overview of Davidson's and other theories of metaphor. Wilson (2006) and Sperber and Wilson (2012)* are excellent expositions of the "echoic" theory of irony, while Currie (2010) ably expounds the pretense theory. Dynel (2013) defends a Gricean approach to irony. Morreal (2012) is an excellent overview of theories of humor, including a fascinating historical lineage, and Attardo (2008) surveys research on the semantics and pragmatics of humor.

References

Aristotle. 1941. *Poetics*. Translated by I. Bywater. In *The Basic Works of Aristotle*, edited by R. McKeon. New York: Random House.
Attardo, S. 2008. "Semantics and Pragmatics of Humor." *Language and Linguistics Compass* 2: 1203–1215.

Bain, A. 1890. *English Composition and Rhetoric*. Enlarged ed. New York: Appleton and Co.

Beardsley, M. 1962. "The Metaphorical Twist." *Philosophy and Phenomenological Research* 22: 293–307.

Camp, E., and Reimer, M. 2006. "Metaphor." In *Oxford Handbook of the Philosophy of Language*, edited by E. Lepore and B. Smith, 846–884. Oxford: Oxford University Press.

Cicero, Quintus Tullius. 1942. *On the Orator, Book II*. Translated by E. W. Sutton and H. Rackham. *Loeb Classical Library*. Cambridge, MA: Harvard University Press.

Currie, G. 1985. "What Is Fiction?" *Journal of Aesthetics and Art Criticism* 43: 385–392.

Currie, G. 2010. *Narratives and Narrators: A Philosophy of Stories*. Oxford: Oxford University Press.

Davidson, D. 1978. "What Metaphors Mean." *Critical Inquiry* 5: 31–47.

Dynel, M. 2013. "Irony from a Neo-Gricean Perspective: On Untruthfulness and Evaluative Implicature." *Intercultural Pragmatics* 10: 403–431.

Green, M. 2017. "Imagery, Expression, and Metaphor." *Philosophical Studies* 174: 33–46.

Grice, P. 1989. *Studies in the Way of Words*. Cambridge, MA: Harvard University Press.

Morreal, J. 2012. "The Philosophy of Humor." In *Stanford Encyclopedia of Philosophy*, edited by Edward Zalta. https://plato.stanford.edu/

Reimer, M. 1996. "The Problem of Dead Metaphor." *Philosophical Studies* 82: 13–25.

Searle, J. 1979. "Metaphor." In *Metaphor and Thought*, edited by A. Ortony, 83–111. Cambridge: Cambridge University Press.

Sperber, D, 1984. "Verbal Irony: Pretense or Echoic Mention?" *Journal of Experimental Psychology: General,* 113: 130–6.

Stock, K. 2017. *Only Imagine: Fiction, Interpretation, and Imagination*. Oxford: Oxford University Press.

Swift, J. (1729) 2008. "A Modest Proposal." In *A Modest Proposal and Other Short Stories Including A Tale of a Tub*, edited by J. Manis, 5–12. University Park: Penn State University Press.

Taylor, J. (1650) 1847. "Of Holy Living." In *Works*, edited by C. Eden. London: Longman, Green.

Tenny, C., Call, J., and Tomasello, M. 2009. "Ratcheting up the Ratchet: On the Evolution of Cumulative Culture." *Philosophical Transactions of the Royal Society, B* 364: 2405–2415.

Vlastos, G. 1987. "Socratic Irony." *The Classical Quarterly* 37: 79–96.

Wilson, D. 2006. "The Pragmatics of Verbal Irony: Echo or Pretence?" *Lingua* 116: 1722–1743.

Wilson, D., and Sperber, D. 2012. "Explaining Irony." In *Meaning and Relevance*, 123–145.

Eleven Features
of Communicative Meaning

CM1.   Some words and sentences are meaningful; others are not.
CM2.   Linguistic meaning is productive.
CM3.   Words, phrases, and sentences are sometimes ambiguous.
CM4.   In language, we may distinguish between types and tokens.
CM5.   Words, phrases, and sentences may be either used or mentioned.
CM6.   What a speaker says sometimes depends on the context in which she says it.
CM7.   In some cases, bits of language can refer to objects—even objects that don't exist.
CM8.   In some cases, bits of language can be true, and in other cases they can be false.
CM9.   Two distinct bits of language can say the same thing.
CM10.   Some bits of language stand in inferential and other "logical" relations to others.
CM11.   Users of language often imply things in a way not captured by the relation of entailment.

GLOSSARY

....

Analytic/synthetic distinction: A distinction, associated with logical empiricism, between those sentences that are true by virtue of the meanings of the terms they contain (analytic), and those that are true but not analytic (synthetic).

A priori: A proposition that is known, or at least knowable, without any recourse to sensory experience.

A posteriori: A proposition that can only be known by recourse to sensory experience.

Biconditional sentence: A sentence of the form 'A if and only if B.'

Character: A semantic property of expressions defined as a function from contexts of utterance to contents.

Common ground: A proposition P is an element of common ground among a group of interlocutors just in case P is (a) accepted by all members of that group, and (b) all members of that group are aware that they all accept P.

Conditional sentence: A sentence of the form, 'If A, then B.'

Conjunctive sentence: A sentence of the form, 'A and B.'

Conversational maxims: A set of norms posited by Grice to help explain how speakers can mean more than, or something distinct from, what they say.

Content: A semantic property of expressions defined as a function from indices to extensions.

Context: A context (or context of utterance) is an abstract characterization of the situation in which an expression is uttered. For purposes of analyzing indexicality, contexts are normally construed as comprising such parameters as the speaker, audience, time, and location.

Context-sensitive: An expression is context-sensitive just in case its content depends on the context in which it is used.

Counterfactual: A sentence of the form, 'If A had been the case, then B would have been the case.'

Demonstrative: An indexical expression which in the most basic case requires a pointing gesture to secure a content. Paradigm examples of demonstratives are 'this' and 'that.'

Designator; rigid, flexible: A rigid designator is a term that refers to the same object across all possible worlds in which that objects exits. A flexible designator is a designator that is not rigid.

Description: A phrase of the form 'a soandso' (indefinite description) or of the form 'the soandso' (definite description).

Descriptive Theory of Proper Names (DTPN): The doctrine that the meaning of a proper name is given by a set of descriptions, which are normally understood as uniquely characterizing the referent of the name. DTPN is one way of elucidating Frege's notion of sense.

Direct reference: The doctrine that the meaning of a proper name is given entirely by its bearer.

Disjunctive sentence: A sentence of the form 'A or B.'

Domain of Discourse: The set of objects over which quantifiers range. That set is often taken to be smaller than the set of all exiting objects, in order to make sense of everyday uses of such phrases as 'all the beer,' which do not normally refer to all of that liquid in the universe.

Entailment: A relation that holds between two propositions A and B just in case any possible situation in which A is true is also one in which B is true.

Explicature: A pragmatic process by which a word or phrase is imbued with a semantic content with the help of pragmatic factors, but in way that goes beyond the more familiar process of saturation.

Expression of a psychological state: A behavior or trait expresses a psychological state just in case it is designed to convey information about that state.

Extension: The semantic value of an expression at a point of evaluation.

Force (illocutionary): Illocutionary force is the way in which content is speaker-meant. Examples include, as an assertion, as a warning, or as a promise.

Generic: A quantificational sentence lacking explicit quantificational expressions. Examples are 'Ravens are black' and 'Men don't ask for directions.'

Illocutionary act: An act of speaker-meaning a content with a particular illocutionary force.

Implicature (conventional, conversational): Implicature is the phenomenon in which a speaker means more, or something different, from what she says. Conventional implicature is due to the meanings of the expressions used, while conversational implicature depends on the interaction among an utterance, maxims governing conversation, and the intentions of the speaker.

Incompatibility: Two sentences are incompatible just in case both cannot be true simultaneously.

Indexical: An expression whose content, or intension, varies systematically with the context in which it is uttered.

Intension: A function from worlds to extensions.

Intention-based semantics: The project of answering the in-virtue-of-what question about linguistic meaning by appeal to speakers' intentions and the conventions that might grow out of patterns of communicative behavior.

Linguistic meaning: An expression has linguistic meaning just in case it has a relatively stable capacity to be used for saying things.

Locutionary act: An act of uttering a meaningful expression.

Natural meaning: An object or state of affairs A carries natural meaning just in case it licenses statements of the form, 'A means B', where B is a distinct object or state of affairs. Meaning in this usage is factive, in that if A does in fact mean B, then B obtains or exists.

Negation (negated sentence): A sentence of the form 'It is not the case that A.'

Negative existential: A sentence of the form 'x does not exist' or, alternatively, 'x's do not exist.'

Organic meaning: An entity or process bears organic meaning just in case it was designed to carry information about a distinct entity or process. The design in question may, but need not, be the result of anyone's intentions.

Performative utterance: An utterance that makes explicit the illocutionary force with which it is made; usually expressed in the first-person indicative active.

Perlocutionary act: The characteristic consequence of an illocutionary act.

Polysemy: A form of ambiguity in which a word's multiple meanings are non–arbitrarily related to one another.

Possible world: A way in which things could be. (The actual world is one of many possible.)

Presupposition (semantic, pragmatic): A sentence S semantically presupposes P just in case P's truth is a condition of S's having a truth value. Pragmatic presupposition is by contract characterized in terms of what speakers take for granted in their utterances.

Principle of Charity: A constraint on the interpretation of an agent's behavior (including her verbal behavior) enjoining us to favor those interpretations that present the agent as on the whole rational.

Productivity of meaning: The observation that with a finite number of words and syntactic operations, speakers are able to produce meaningful strings with no apparent upper bound on their complexity.

Projectile: An expression e is a projectile just in case its user incurs a commitment regardless of how deeply embedded e is within other expressions.

Quantifier: An expression typically used to help answer a question of the form how many? or how much?

Semantic compositionality: The doctrine that the linguistic meaning of a complex expression depends in a systematic way upon the linguistic meanings of the expressions from which it is built, together with the means by which it is built from them. (Semantic Compositionality comes in a stronger and a weaker form.)

Semantics: The study of linguistic meaning.

Silencing (illocutionary): A putative illocutionary act is silenced just in case a pattern of malfeasance on the part of the speaker, or of injustice in her social milieu, cause the illocutionary act she aims to perform, instead to misfire.

Slur: An expression used to denigrate its referent on account of that referent's membership in a particular group.

Speaker meaning (a.k.a. nonnatural meaning): A form of communicative meaning in which an agent performs an act with an intention of making a commitment of hers overt, or of producing a psychological state in another agent by means of that agent's recognition of her intention.

Synonymy: Two expressions are synonymous just in case they have the same linguistic meaning.

Theory of Mind (ToM): An appreciation that an agent has that other individuals distinct from herself have psychological states, and that those states might be different from her own.

Truth-conditional semantics: The doctrine that the linguistic meaning of a sentence may be captured by its truth conditions.

Use and mention: An expression might occur in the performance of a speech act, or by itself being referred to. Quotation marks are often, but not necessarily, used in mentioning uses.

INDEX

....